Realization

Dedicated to:
Jim,
Nana,
and
4 girls and 5 boys . . .
who are most important in my life!
Lyn

Dedicated to:
Mom,
7 boys,
and
91 years later,
Michael

Realization

The Change Imperative for Deepening District-Wide Reform

Lyn Sharratt
Michael Fullan

Foreword by Kenneth Leithwood

A JOINT PUBLICATION

CORWIN
A SAGE Company

ONTARIO
PRINCIPALS'
COUNCIL
Exemplary Leadership
in Public Education

For information:

Corwin
A SAGE Company
2455 Teller Road
Thousand Oaks, California 91320
(800) 233-9936
Fax: (800) 417-2466
www.corwinpress.com

SAGE India Pvt. Ltd.
B 1/I 1 Mohan Cooperative
  Industrial Area
Mathura Road, New Delhi 110 044
India

SAGE Ltd.
1 Oliver's Yard
55 City Road
London EC1Y 1SP
United Kingdom

SAGE Asia-Pacific Pte. Ltd.
33 Pekin Street #02-01
Far East Square
Singapore 048763

Printed in the United States of America.

Library of Congress Cataloging-in-Publication Data

Sharratt, Lyn.
Realization: the change imperative for deepening district-wide reform/Lyn Sharratt, Michael Fullan.
       p. cm.
"A Joint Publication With the Ontario Principals' Council."
Includes bibliographical references and index.
ISBN 978-1-4129-7385-4 (pbk.)
    1. School management and organization. 2. School improvement programs.
3. School districts. I. Fullan, Michael. II. Ontario Principals' Council. III. Title.

LB2805.S578 2009
371.2'07—dc22   2009023341

This book is printed on acid-free paper.

09   10   11   12   13   10   9   8   7   6   5   4   3   2   1

Acquisitions Editor:	Arnis Burvikovs
Associate Editor:	Desirée A. Bartlett
Production Editor:	Cassandra Margaret Seibel
Copy Editor:	Sarah J. Duffy
Typesetter:	C&M Digitals (P) Ltd.
Proofreader:	Susan Schon
Indexer:	Jean Casalegno
Cover Designer:	Michael Dubowe

Contents

List of Figures

Foreword

Realization: The Change Imperative for Deepening District-Wide Reform is one of those books that gives me great encouragement that large-scale reform is indeed possible. Lyn Sharratt and Michael Fullan show how ordinary people, using what we know and applying it with insight and persistence, can accomplish great things. This book furnishes a clear and compelling account of how whole-system reform can be achieved.

Public schooling is a mass production enterprise. I do not intend by this phrase anything mechanical, linear, or industrial—quite the contrary. I mean only that it is large scale in almost all political jurisdictions, involving millions of students, thousands of staff, billions of dollars, and a great deal of real estate. Such a mass production enterprise cannot depend for most of its success on a small proportion of exceptionally talented or exceptionally committed people. Although these people, able to accomplish great things against all odds, should always be supported and will often make important differences.

But the enterprise, day to day, needs to function acceptably well when it is staffed by a relatively normal distribution of the adult population. The work they are expected to do needs to be achievable—and achievable with realistic amounts of effort and talent. The odds need to be stacked in favor, not against, their success. Indeed, the achievements of our current schools probably represent what can reasonably be achieved under the circumstances in which they find themselves.

Contrary to the views of many, the prevailing model for "doing school" is an enormously adaptive response to the mass production demands placed on it. Few social organizations can match the durability of schools. They are sensitively aligned to the terms and conditions of the social contract that exists between them and the publics they serve. It is the sensitivity of that alignment that accounts for the durability (some would say inertia) of schooling, as we know it, in the face of considerable criticism and persistent efforts to reform.

The terms of that social contract are many, extending far beyond helping children learn what is outlined in the official curriculum. While such learning is clearly the centerpiece, the contract also includes, for example, child care, community building, and surrogate parenting. In addition, the contract stipulates the resources available for the work, places constraints on how those resources are to be used, and prescribes most of the institutional arrangements within which schooling will take place. It is these more comprehensive terms of the social contract that account for much of what reformers would like to change.

But it is rare indeed for reformers to significantly challenge or change most terms of the social contract in order to realize their preferred goals. Their efforts, rather, are best described as tinkering around the edges of the contract, tweaking the standard model of schooling, or, quite frequently, creating aspirational goals for student learning with little or no realistic consideration of how the other terms of the social contact would need to change for schools to actually realize such goals. As bizarre as it seems, on those occasions when the terms of the social contract are significantly changed, the changes are as likely to make it harder rather than easier for those in schools to hold up their end of the bargain—providing less rather than more discretion to get the job done, less rather than more time to thoughtfully prepare for the learning of one's students, fewer rather than more resources, and the like.

On a recent visit to Naples, Florida, I ran across two articles on education in the same edition of the local paper.[1] The article on page 9B, headlined "Fla. High School Graduation Standards May Increase," described a bill expected to be passed by the state legislature (and strongly backed by Florida's business community) that would "increase math and science requirements and raise the passing grade for the 10th grade Florida Comprehensive Assessment Test [FCAT]." The article on page 3B carried the headline "Lee Board Urges Parents to Speak Loudly Against Drastic Budget Cuts."[2] It described the difficulties about to be faced by one of the local school districts because of the roughly $60 to $80 million anticipated shortfall in state allocations to the district for the 2009–2010 budget year. According to this article, such cuts could only be accommodated by eliminating 578 positions, cancelling all art and music programs, and making many other across-the-board cuts.

One need not have scored level 2 on the FCAT[3] to see how these two sets of events are related; "misaligned" would be putting it mildly, and "dreaming in technicolor" might be a good description of the legislators' state of mind. But as obvious as this misalignment would seem to be, other cases are depressingly easy to find. So this book by Lyn Sharratt and Michael Fullan comes as a great relief to people like me who believe that most public schools do a remarkable job of education within the constraints imposed by their social contracts, as they are typically constructed, and could do a much better job if some of the terms of that social contract were significantly altered.

The work described in this book provides compelling evidence that when schools are provided with opportunities to significantly increase their resources—in this case, primarily the skills and knowledge of teachers, administrators, and parents—their students are the big winners. This is the case, at least, when considerable effort is made to ensure that other terms of the social contract are modified and aligned in light of this increased capacity and the effort that it requires. But the district-wide (and eventually province-wide) project described in this book goes far beyond justifying these important claims. It illustrates, in ways that seem largely portable to other district contexts, what it takes beyond increasing the district's capacities to realize the changes in practice made possible by those new capacities.

These lessons about realization go the heart of school improvement; they also help explain why so many well-intentioned large-scale reform efforts produce disappointing results. These are lessons about the importance of uncommon amounts of persistence in the face of competing priorities, unfailing attention to the details of implementation, hard-nosed decisions about how best to allocate scarce resources, ego-free leadership, and ongoing attention to evidence about what is working and what needs to be modified. Realization, this book shows us quite convincingly, is not for the faint of heart or the impatient. This book has critical messages for those aiming to actually help schools do a better job for their students and should be required reading for anyone with that goal in mind.

Kenneth Leithwood

NOTES

1. Kaczor, B., "Fla. High School Graduation Standards May Increase," *Associated Press,* March 25, 2009.

2. Williams, L., "Lee Board Urges Parents to Speak Loudly Against Drastic Budget Cuts," *Naples Daily News,* March 25, 2009.

3. To pass, students need to score at or above level 2 on the five-level FCAT.

Preface

We have been working on district-wide reform for over 30 years, and on whole-system reform (province, state, country) since 1997. In the course of this work, capacity building has come to play a central role—strategies that develop individual and collective knowledge, competencies, and dispositions essential for improvement of student learning.

In this book we delve more specifically and comprehensively into what capacity building looks like and how to achieve more of it—what we call the nitty-gritty of doing it. This is important in its own right because the term *capacity building* can easily become superficial and vague in its use.

But we have a deeper interest and purpose, which is how to institutionalize and sustain capacity building for every teacher and every student—what we call realization—the 14th parameter that crystallizes the environment created by satisfying the demands of the other 13 parameters that formed the basis of our original model. Thus having worked with capacity building for two decades, the next strategy question is how to embed it in large systems.

In Chapter 1 we set the frame by reviewing the main core elements of capacity building and its relationship to realization. Chapter 2 talks about the nitty-gritty of capacity building, and Chapter 3 is about the day-to-day modeling, sharing, and guiding of effective practice.

In Chapter 4 we consolidate system-wide capacity building as interdependent practice, or realization. It is here that we introduce the system as a whole, including the role of the state or province. In Chapter 5 we worry about the barriers to going deeper, and in Chapter 6 we take up the question of whole-system reform involving the school, district, and state levels as a means of sustaining realization.

This book melds theory and practice. We have always had a strong knowledge base, but theory is advanced best through purposeful action. We can no longer tell where theory begins and practice ends or vice versa. When the system has achieved realization, theory and practice become seamless.

Acknowledgments

W e are grateful to the many literacy leaders who have worked continuously to make sustainable improvements for our students in the York Region District School Board (YRDSB). All this would not be possible except for the inspiring, knowledgeable, participatory leadership of Bill Hogarth, director of education/CEO of YRDSB. With the support of trustees, Bill weathered tough times, always staying the course of increasing students' literacy achievement by modeling true commitment and shared beliefs and understandings at every turn.

We thank the staff members of Curriculum and Instructional Services, YRDSB, the front-line literacy experts who continue to work with an urgent moral imperative that models knowledge, tireless support, and availability to all staff. Beate Planche and her staff continue to work as a unified, highly competent team across the system alongside field superintendents, administrators, and literacy coaches to demonstrate what the 13 parameters look like in classrooms when fully implemented so that *all* students are achieving.

Principals, vice principals, literacy coaches, and classroom teachers—elementary and secondary—in YRDSB are extraordinary! They take risks and continuously refine high-yield assessment and instructional strategies to ensure that learning happens for our students. They are caring and respectful, and they continue to define what is possible as a community of learners.

Superintendents in YRDSB continue to take our work more deeply into classrooms to reach all 8,800 teachers and their 130,000 students. They actively show that their first priority is to increase students' literacy achievement. Field superintendents are truly and rightfully proud of their schools' teams, especially when they hear the improvement articulated at the annual Literacy Learning Fair. Divisional superintendents are equally proud to be on focus by annually presenting their department improvement plans that focus on students' achievement to the elected board.

Kenneth Leithwood has worked with both of us at the Ontario Institute for Studies in Education at the University of Toronto for many years. We value his wisdom and his scholarly and thought-provoking research. His ongoing research in YRDSB in the areas of transformational and distributed leadership continues to set a high and clearly defined standard for us. He always has time to reflect on our journey as a true mentor to us and to our colleagues in the district.

The Literacy and Numeracy Secretariat staff of the Ontario Ministry of Education has been supportive of the focused work in YRDSB for many years. They have provided insights and funding that have helped us do what we knew had to be done in order to reach each stage of our strategic implementation.

PUBLISHER'S ACKNOWLEDGMENTS

Corwin gratefully acknowledges the contribution of the following individuals:

Toni Callahan
Retired Social Studies Teacher
Westmont Hilltop School District
Johnstown, PA

Sheila Gragg
Technology Integration Coach, Professional Developer
Ashbury College
Nepean, ON, Canada

Patti Grammens
Department Chair, 8th Grade Science Teacher,
Science Olympiad Coach
South Forsyth Middle School
Cumming, GA

Kathy J. Grover
Assistant Superintendent
Curriculum & Instruction
Clever R-V Public Schools
Clever, MO

Joe Ann Hinrichs
Associate Dean for Doctoral Programs
Walden University
Richard W. Riley College of Education and Leadership
Thomasville, GA

Dan Kortvelesy
Curriculum Supervisor
Math, Technology, Business Education, Media
Mainland Regional High School
Linwood, NJ

Patricia Long Tucker
Regional Superintendent
District of Columbia Public Schools
Washington, DC

Monica Uphoff
Director of Assessment
Coppell Independent School District
Coppell, TX

Shawn White
Social Science Chair
Weston McEwen High School
Athena, OR

About the Authors

Lyn Sharratt taught elementary- and secondary-aged students in regular and special needs classrooms for 22 years in three jurisdictions in Ontario before beginning her career in educational administration. She became administrator and associate professor at York University's Faculty of Education, was an executive assistant responsible for professional development at a provincial (state) teachers' union, and from 1992 to 1995 was director of curriculum and program for the provincial association, OPSBA, representing 1,100 publicly elected trustees.

Lyn then became a field superintendent for York Region District School Board (YRDSB) in 1995 and in 1996 earned a doctorate from Ontario Institute for Studies in Education at the University of Toronto (OISE/UT). Following seven years in the field, she was named superintendent of curriculum and instructional services. Currently, Lyn is senior advisor of system and school improvement in YRDSB, coordinating external research focused on increasing student achievement. She is also an associate at OISE/UT, supervising doctoral students in the Department of Theory and Policy Studies. Visit her website at www.lynsharratt.com.

Michael Fullan is professor emeritus at the Ontario Institute for Studies in Education at the University of Toronto. Recognized as an international authority on large-scale reform, he is engaged in training, advising, and evaluating large projects around the world. His work is driven by the moral purpose of raising the bar and closing the gap for all children.

Michael is the author of many bestselling books, most recently *The Six Secrets of Change, Turnaround Leadership for Higher Education,* and *The Challenge of Change.* Visit his website at www .michaelfullan.ca.

CHAPTER ONE

Capacity Building

A Journey of Deepening Discovery

Since about 1990 there has been a growing body of work that points to common characteristics and strategies that successful school districts use to raise student achievement. In Rosenholtz's (1989) study of 78 elementary schools, she classified schools as "stuck," "moving," and "in-between." She also found that a disproportionate number of stuck schools came from certain districts; likewise, moving schools were clustered in certain other districts. This prompted her to write a chapter on stuck and moving districts (two of the eight districts were in the latter category). Here is an excerpt:

> The contrast between stuck and moving districts, nowhere more apparent than here, underscores how principals become helpful instructional advisors or maladroit managers of their schools. It is also clear that stuck superintendents attribute poor performance to principals themselves, rather than accepting any responsibility to help them learn and improve. This again may indicate their lack of technical knowledge and subsequent threats to their self-esteem. If districts take no responsibility for the inservice needs of principals, of course, principals become less able colleagues, less effective problem solvers, more reluctant to refer school problems to the central office for outside assistance, more threatened by their lack of technical knowledge, and most essential, of substantially less help to teachers. Of equal importance,

with very little helpful assistance, stuck superintendents symbolically communicate the norm of self-reliance—and subsequently professional isolation—that improvement may not be possible, or worthy of their time and effort, or that principals should solve problems by themselves—lugubrious lessons principals may unwittingly hand down to poorly performing teachers, and thus teachers to students. (p. 189)

As we headed into the new century, evidence appeared to be coalescing around what it would take for districts to achieve district-wide success, at least in literacy and numeracy (see Fullan, 2007, Chapter 11). Togneri and Anderson's (2003) study of success in five high-poverty districts found six clear and consistent strategies at work:

1. Publicly acknowledging poor performance and seeking solutions (building the will for reform)

2. Focusing intensively on improving instruction and achievement

3. Building a system-wide framework and infrastructure to support instruction

4. Redefining and distributing leadership at all levels of the district

5. Making professional development relevant and useful

6. Recognizing that there are no quick fixes (p. 13)

Anderson (2006) also reviewed the research on district effectiveness and named 12 key strategic components:

1. District-wide sense of efficacy

2. District-wide focus on student achievement and the quality of instruction

3. Adoption of and commitment to district-wide performance standards

4. Development and adoption of district-wide curriculum approaches to instruction

5. Alignment of curriculum, teaching and learning materials, and assessment to relevant standards

6. Multimeasure accountability systems and system-wide use of data to inform practice, hold school and district leaders accountable for results, and monitor progress

7. Targets and phased focuses of improvement

8. Investment in instructional leadership development at the school and district levels

9. District-wide, job-embedded professional development foci and supports for teachers

10. District-wide and school-level emphasis on teamwork and professional community (including, in several cases, positive partnerships with unions)

11. New approaches to board-district relations and in-district relations

12. Strategic relations with state reform policies and resources

One would think, then, that we have a growing consensus on the key factors for success and that it is just a matter of going to town on what we know. Such are the subtleties and complexities of capacity building that while it seems so obvious, implementation is never straightforward.

NOT SO FAST

So a district should get the standards right, align curriculum to them, conduct assessments on the new alignment, provide solid and continuous professional development on curriculum and instruction, set up a data system that can be used for both assessment *for* and *of* learning, and engage with the local community and state reform policies. It may surprise many readers that these steps by themselves are not sufficient and, at best, may represent a waste of resources or, at worst, do more harm than good.

The experience of the San Diego Unified School District is a good place to start with respect to the "not so fast" theme. Coming off a highly successful experience in District 2 in New York City from 1988 to 1996, Tony Alvarado was hired as chancellor of instruction in 1997 to join a new high-profile superintendent, Alan Bersin, in San Diego. In a sense the question was, if you could take the best knowledge and add resources and political clout, could you get results in a large urban district within a four-year period and then keep going, in this case moving from success in 45 schools (District 2 in New York) to 175 schools (San Diego)? The answer, incidentally, is yes, but it would require good strategies and a good deal of finesse, which as it turned out were not present in the San Diego strategy.

The San Diego story is one of the most closely watched reform initiatives in the history of urban school improvement. We draw here on the excellent account by Hubbard, Mehan, and Stein (2006). The San Diego strategy was well detailed and explicit from day one and consisted of three components:

1. Improved student learning: closing the achievement gap

2. Improved instruction: teacher learning through professional development

3. Restructuring the organization to support student learning and instruction

The focus was on literacy, and the strategies, highly specific. Teachers received support from literacy coaches and principals who were positioned to be "leaders of instruction," with day-to-day support and monthly full-day inservice sessions by area superintendents whose new role (and new people) was re-created as that of instructional leader.

We don't need to discuss in detail the San Diego experience, but the main outcomes and reasons can be identified (for a full account, see Hubbard et al., 2006). To cut to the chase, literacy achievement increased somewhat at the elementary level in the 1997–2001 period, increased very little in middle schools, and failed dismally in high schools. Momentum was lost by 2001, Alvarado was asked to leave in 2002, and Bersin, after slowing down the nature and pace of reform in 2003–2004, was replaced by the school board when his term expired in June 2005. What happened?

One could say that it was a political problem—the board was divided from the beginning (three to two in favor of the reform initiative), and the teacher union that opposed the reform from the beginning eventually carried the day. There is some truth to this, but the deeper explanation comes closer to the theme of our interest in meaning and motivation, the "too tight/too loose" problem, and the depth of instructional change and thinking required to make a difference. Hubbard and colleagues (2006) expressed the basic problem in terms of three challenges that the strategy failed to address: "the need to accomplish deep learning within the constraints of a limited time frame, principals' and coaches' limited understanding of the concepts that they were trying to teach, and the difficulty of reaching common ground between school leaders and teachers" (p. 128).

All this despite plenty of classroom visits, walk-throughs involving all schools, frequent problem-solving sessions, and an emphasis on job-embedded professional learning. The San Diego case is an exercise in the dilemmas faced by leaders with an urgent sense of moral purpose and considerable knowledge of what should happen in classroom instruction. But it also points to how the strategies employed must be more respectful of how deep change happens. Much good was done in improving literacy achievement in elementary schools, but it was not deep enough or "owned enough" to go further. The San Diego strategy failed because the pace of change was too fast, the strategy was too unidirectional from the top, relationships were not built with teachers and principals, and above all, the strategies did not really build capacity, which is the development of collective knowledge and understandings required for ongoing instructional improvement that meets the needs of each child. This is going to be a lot harder than we thought.

The purpose of our book is not only to map out capacity building more clearly, but also to suggest that even this will not be sufficient. We need to go from strong capacity building to what we call *realization.*

Another confirmation of our "not so fast" worry (reminds us of the Latin adage *festina lente*—hasten slowly) comes from the Cross City Campaign for Urban School Reform (2005), which examined major reform initiatives in Chicago, Milwaukee, and Seattle. All three school systems had the attention of political leaders at all levels of the system and focused on the "right things" such as literacy and math; all three systems used current choice strategies such as concentration on "assessment for learning" data, invested heavily in professional development, developed new leadership, and focused on system-wide change.

And they had money—Seattle had $35 million in external funds, Milwaukee had extra resources and flexibility, and Chicago had multimillions. There was huge pressure, but success was not expected overnight. Decision makers and the public would have been content to see growing success over a 5- or even 10-year period. The upfront conclusion of the case evaluators was that, as many of the principals and teachers interviewed saw it, "the districts were unable to change and improve practice on a large scale" (Cross City Campaign for Urban School Reform, 2005, p. 4).

The issues in the Chicago, Milwaukee, and Seattle reforms help identify the missing ingredient, even though those districts appear to have gotten most components right. Chicago, for example, appeared to have an impressive strategy: "Academic standards and instructional frameworks, assessment and accountability systems, and professional development for standards-based instruction are among the tools of systemic reform that are used to change classroom instruction" (Cross City Campaign for Urban School Reform, 2005, p. 23). Here is standards-based system-wide reform that sounds like it should work. The failure, we think, is that the strategy lacked a focus on what needed to change in instructional practice. In Chicago, teachers did focus on standards, but in interviews they "did not articulate any deep changes in teaching practices that may have been underway" (p. 23). Furthermore, "instructional goals were articulated more often in terms of student outcomes or achievement levels than in terms of instructional quality, that is *what the schools do* to help students achieve" (p. 29, emphasis in original).

Milwaukee reveals similar problems in achieving instructional improvements while using greater decentralization in the context of system support and competitive choice. The focus was on literacy; a literacy coach was housed in every school in the district, and considerable professional development and technical support services were available. Education plans for each school were to focus on literacy standards through (1) data analysis and assessment and (2) subject-area achievement targets, including literacy across the curriculum. Sounds like a convincing strategy. However, what is missing, again, is the black box of instructional practice in all classrooms. The case writers observe: "We placed the Education Plan in the indirect category due to its non-specificity regarding regular or desired instructional content and practices" (Cross City Campaign for Urban School Reform, 2005, p. 49). More generally, the report concludes that while these serious district-wide reform initiatives appeared to prioritize instruction, they did so indirectly (through standards, assessment, leadership responsibilities). However, in the experience of principals and teachers, the net effect was that "policies and signals were non-specific regarding intended effects on classroom teaching and learning" (p. 65).

Our third case, Seattle, is a variation on the same theme. The game plan looks good. Standards defined the direction, while the district's Transformational Academic Achievement Planning Process "was designed as a vehicle for (1) helping students meet standards, and (2) eliminating the achievement gap between white students and students of color" (Cross City Campaign for Urban School Reform, 2005, p. 66). Like Milwaukee, Seattle reorganized to support site-based management, including the allocation of considerable resources to schools. The case writers observe: "The recent effort to become a standards-based district was one of the first sustained instructional reform efforts with direct attention to teaching and learning. However, the conversations district leaders had about standards *were rarely connected to changes in instruction"* (p. 69, emphasis added). The report continues: "At the school level, finding teachers who understood the implications of standards for their teaching was difficult" (p. 72).

We cite one more case, which in some ways is more encouraging but still proves our main conclusion that instructional change is going to require different strategies that help shape collective capacity and shared commitment to engage in continuous improvement. Supovitz (2006) conducted an excellent case study of the reform effort in Duval County, Florida. The title of his book captures the emphasis of his analysis: *The Case for District-Based Reform.* Supovitz chronicled the district-wide reform effort from 1999 through 2005. The reform strategy is now familiar to us.

1. Develop a specific vision of what high-quality instruction should look like

2. Build both the commitment and capacity of employees across the system to enact and support the instructional vision

3. Construct mechanisms to provide data at all levels of the system that will be used both to provide people with information that informs their practices and to monitor the implementation of the instructional vision

4. Develop the means to help people continually deepen their implementation and to help the district continually refine this vision and understand its implications

With a sustained five-year focus on these four strategic components, the district made significant gains in student achievement. For example, the number of schools receiving a C or better on the state assessment system went from 87 (of 142) in 1999 to 121 by 2003. Also, for the first time in seven years, in 2005 no school received an F on the state accountability system.

The strategy was driven by a strong superintendent who helped orchestrate the development of district-wide capacity according to the four core components. The strategy was enacted with considerable action and focus. As Supovitz (2006) reports, "Duval County leaders repeatedly stated their vision and the strategies for achieving it in public venues" (p. 43). He argues that the spread and deepening of district-wide success is as much "gardening" as it is "engineering" (p. 63), and that the balance requires "advocacy without mandate" (p. 66), "fostering urgency" (p. 68), and "building existing proof" of success (p. 69). We see a similar array of strategies in San Diego, but with less heavy-handedness: direct training of teachers, school standards coaches, district standards coaches, principals' instructional leadership development, and district leadership development.

With six years of consistent effort and an explicit emphasis on professional learning communities as a strategy, "the possibilities of professional learning communities—rigorous inquiry into the problems and challenges of instructional practice and the support of that practice—seemed only to be occurring in pockets of the district" (Supovitz, 2006, p. 174). Much was accomplished in Duval County, but it was by no means deep or durable. So our "not so fast" worry is apt. Even with comprehensive strategies and a relentless focus over a five- to six-year period, we are still not getting it right.

CAPACITY BUILDING TO REALIZATION

The good news, then, is that school districts have realized that capacity building is the key to successful school improvement. We define *capacity building* as investment in the development of the knowledge, skills, and competencies of individuals and groups to focus on assessment literacy and instructional effectiveness that leads to school improvement. What districts have not realized is that capacity building is only a good start. The real goal is converting it to full implementation or what we call *realization*. Capacity building must become systemic if it is going to make a performance difference for all schools in a district. The quest for realization via systemic capacity building—broad (every school) and deep (every classroom)—is the subject of this book.

Capacity building, a highly complex, dynamic, knowledge-building process, is intended to lead to increased student achievement in every school. To achieve that goal, consideration must be given to approaches that will result in systemic capacity building. And the key to driving this successful systemic capacity building—full realization in every classroom by which we will succeed in improving all schools for all students—is knowledge building that is universally aligned and coherent, knowledge building that emanates both from the center and the field simultaneously and in concert.

We have worked in many different districts across North America and beyond on district-wide capacity building. Our most intensive and extensive work has been in York Region District School Board (YRDSB), where one of us (Sharratt) was superintendent of curriculum and instruction designing and leading the strategy from within and the other (Fullan) served as external consultant and researcher.

We use YRDSB as one detailed case, but the ideas are entirely consistent with the pursuit of district-wide reform that we reviewed in the previous section of this chapter. YRDSB is a large multicultural region immediately north of Toronto, Ontario. It has over 130,000 students and 8,800 teachers in its 161 elementary and 31 secondary schools. More than 100 languages are spoken in the schools, and there is a steady stream of immigrants entering YRDSB schools every month of the school year. Student achievement in Ontario is assessed through criterion-referenced assessments for all children in Grades 3, 6, 9, and 10 conducted by an independent agency, the Education and Quality Accountability Office (EQAO). The district's reform, driven by a focus on literacy, unfolded in the context of a province-wide strategy that commenced in 2003.

The journey began in 1999 after the director of education (superintendent/CEO), Bill Hogarth, had shocked the system by stating that "all students will read by the end of Grade 1." A provocative challenge that begged the question: How would this be accomplished? This book is an account of how the district successfully implemented capacity building across its schools, discovering along the way that this is not sufficient for deep, sustainable reform.

YRDSB started with four big-picture, enduring understandings that would form the foundation of systemic capacity building:

- Commitment to the shared vision and staying the course with a singular priority—literacy
- Knowledge of and resources for focused assessment linked to instruction at all levels

- Strategic leadership emanating simultaneously and consistently from the center and the field, and politically
- Engagement of parents and community—involvement so schools become theirs (L. Sharratt, 1996, 2001)

These broad strokes are expanded in the remainder of this chapter. It is important to note that we have intentionally used the term *professional learning* (PL) over the more narrow conceptual terms *professional development* and *professional learning communities* (Fullan, Hill, & Crévola, 2006) because our work here is about focused, ongoing learning—for, with, and on behalf of every teacher and student. In the course of this book, we will move from the broad picture to the nitty-gritty of capacity building, into systemic capacity building, ultimately achieving realization.

Commitment to a Shared Vision

Teachers change practices when the school district is committed to a single priority, vision, or belief that is supported by PL. Teachers feel that inservice training is essential to their learning, especially when principals support and participate in the PL (L. Sharratt, 1996, p. 100). We have found that focusing deeply on only one goal, such as literacy (including mathematical literacy), with teachers and administrators is necessary—even urgent—in order to create passion, commitment, and a zeal for teaching and learning. Commitment from system leaders, administrators, and teachers to a single, shared vision is what we call *the moral imperative.*

Focused Assessment and Instructional Practices

In order to increase achievement, teachers need an expanded repertoire of instructional practices reflective of valid formative assessment data that together form an accurate, integrated image of each learner. Practices used need to embrace, for example, data-driven whole-group, small-group, and individual learning; structured group work; focused time on task; and uninterrupted blocks of instructional time.

Strategic Leadership

Teachers feel that leadership influences their learning, and they change practices most when leadership is strategic. This includes leadership in school planning that encompasses developing a shared vision that is aligned with the district vision; uses collaborative decision-making processes; establishes a collective, problem-solving environment; ensures flexible school structures; and gives time and support to teachers. *Strategic* implies knowledge of and commitment to shared beliefs and understandings and intentional teaching of *all* students.

Parental and Community Involvement

Research reveals that families who are involved in their children's schooling significantly increase these students' performance (Epstein, 1995). By taking a collaborative approach to the development of family-involvement programs, schools can form successful partnerships with families and community groups to improve the educational achievement of all students. "With frequent interactions among school, families, and communities," notes Epstein, "more students are more likely to receive common messages from various people about the importance of school, of working hard, of thinking creatively, of helping one another, and of staying in school" (p. 701). As a result, school-family-community partnerships enable students and families to produce their own successes.

Some commentators on public education make a point that student performance in any school is the direct effect of socioeconomic measures in the school area—the higher the status, the higher the scores. This myth has been shattered many times, especially by results from schools in challenging circumstances where administrators' and teachers' knowledge of each learner, precise assessment and instruction, and concerted efforts to involve parents and community have made remarkable differences for all students.

If these four broad conditions of system and school improvement are so important, as authors we ask: How can we put wheels under them to move a district forward? We are great advocates of learning by (reflective) doing. The sooner you get to purposeful action, the greater the skill development, the greater the clarity, and the more authentic the shared ownership. We know the foundation and the direction, but the nitty-gritty of capacity building remains to be discovered.

With all this clarity in research about district-wide reform, it seems to be a mystery why more districts are not becoming successful through the use of these ideas. The answer for us is that it is hard to do, day after day.

One of the six secrets of change is that "learning is the work" (Fullan, 2008, p. 75). Richard Elmore (2008) has observed that, if seeking deep change, people have to learn in the settings in which they work. It turns out that learning in this way, individually and collectively, requires enormous focused and sustained attention to a small set of key factors that are essential for success. If one looks closely at the companies that do this well, such as Toyota and Southwest Airlines, what is striking is that being successful year after year, decade after decade demands concentrated effort by scores of people reinforcing and leveraging each other's efforts. This is why so few organizations do it.

In *Outliers*, Malcolm Gladwell (2008) identifies impressive success in various walks of life as a function of circumstances (opportunity) and sustained hard work—learning more and more through practice, practice, practice. He estimates that to become an expert in a given field requires at least ten thousand hours of dedicated work. Note, Gladwell is talking about individuals succeeding. If we apply this to organizations or systems, we are dealing with collectives. For collectives it has to take at least thirty thousand hours using Gladwell's metric just to get good, and endless hours to sustain this goodness. This is why so few school districts have been able to progress.

So there is no substitute for making "learning is the work" the focal point of everyone's business. No amount of structural changes, resources, professional learning, strategic planning, or charismatic leaders will do the trick. It all starts with the daily grind of laying the foundation through the nitty-gritty of capacity building.

CHAPTER TWO

The Nitty-Gritty of Capacity Building

A ll school districts have great visions—on paper. What most don't have is a systematic strategy for getting there. To create the latter, you need a grounded, comprehensive theory of action. In other words, you need to make the four foundational conditions—shared and focused vision, intentional assessment and instruction, strategic leadership, and engagement of students and community—an experienced reality.

All large-scale reform faces a dilemma: How do you get coherence in an otherwise fragmented system? How do you get shared specificity and consistency of good practice without imposing it (which doesn't work)? If some practices are so effective, how do they come to have the status of "non-negotiable"?

We have learned quite a lot about this problem in the past decade in York Region District School Board (YRDSB), which we have in turn applied to entire systems, that is, all districts in a province (Fullan 2009a; Levin, Glaze, & Fullan, 2008). The short answer is that system leaders provide direction and then set out to fairly rapidly discover the particulars through partnerships or joint pursuits between district leadership and schools, and among schools. The idea is to identify and retain those specific strategies that are causally linked to getting better results.

In YRDSB, a large multicultural district north of Toronto, we established what is called the Literacy Collaborative (LC), which focuses on the single goal of increased literacy achievement for all elementary and secondary students. We identified three powerful and strategic elements of that one goal:

1. Using data to drive instruction and the selection of resources

2. Building administrators' and teachers' capacity for focused literacy assessment and literacy instruction

3. Establishing professional learning communities across all schools to share successful practice

One full year was spent vetting the definition of *literacy,* ensuring that all those involved had an opportunity to comment on it and see themselves in it. The important points are that literacy encompasses mathematics and expresses, with clarity, how it begins and what it must become. This definition (YRDSB, 2007a) later became embedded in policy:

Literacy is the development of a continuum of skills, knowledge and attitudes that prepare all of our learners for life in a changing world community. It *begins* with the fundamental acquisition of skills in reading, writing, listening, speaking, viewing, representing, responding and *mathematics.* It *becomes* the ability to understand, think, apply and communicate effectively in all subject and program areas in a variety of ways and for a variety of purposes. (p. 2)

We then set out to jointly determine and retain the particular substrategies that would accomplish the LC goal on the ground. Those substrategies came to be known as the 13 parameters (see Figure 2.1), and they are in effect the nitty-gritty of capacity building. Think of these parameters as the specific strategies that, in combination, "cause" classroom, school, and district improvement.

It is important to note that the 13 parameters were generated jointly by district and school leaders (including teachers) through research and discussion. As they are identified and stand the test of evidence and practicality, they are retained, reviewed, and embedded in the district. It is a long story, but through district professional learning (PL) sessions, consultant workshops, team-based capacity building, evidence-based refinement from within the YRDSB experience, and from the wider literature, the parameters have come to have a named status. Leaders throughout the system come to walk

Figure 2.1 The 13 Parameters

1. Shared beliefs and understandings

2. Embedded literacy coaches

3. Time-tabled literacy block

4. Principal leadership

5. Early and ongoing intervention

6. Case management approach

7. Literacy professional development at school staff meetings

8. In-school grade/subject meetings

9. Book rooms with leveled books and resources

10. Allocation of district and school budgets for literacy learning and resources

11. Action research focused on literacy

12. Parental involvement

13. Cross-curricular literacy connections

Source: L. Sharratt & Fullan, 2005, 2006.

the talk and equally, simultaneously talk the walk—strategies are geared to learning about implementation during implementation. This *implementation as learning* serves to further specify the meaning of each component and its efficacy in developing capacity. Implementation as learning blurs the theory-practice lines, further embedding successes and moving the district toward realization.

All 192 YRDSB schools (in four cohorts because of sheer numbers), including all elementary and secondary schools, and principals as lead-learners participate as teams in capacity-building sessions that focus on the 13 parameters in action. The director (superintendent/CEO), Bill Hogarth, attends these sessions—participating and often presenting with Sharratt—as the "chief learning officer." This is not his official title, but one he executes daily and wears proudly, as he should. Additional strategies, in between district-led sessions, give people time to experience and get support in their implementation. These include literacy coach training, demonstration classrooms, time-tabled common planning time, literacy walks, schools working in clusters focused on assessment and instruction, and so on (see Resource B, p. 106).

THE 13 PARAMETERS IN DETAIL

The parameters, then, come to have specific meaning through the experience of implementing them. The following elaborates on their particulars.

1. Shared beliefs and understandings. Leaders in schools must believe and take action to demonstrate that they commit to the following:

   a. All students can achieve high standards, given sufficient time and the right support.
   b. High expectations and early and ongoing intervention are essential.
   c. All teachers can teach to high standards given the right assistance.
   d. Teachers need to be able to articulate what they teach and why they teach the way they do. (adapted from Hill & Crévola, 1999)

Strategic leaders, from the members of the elected Board of Trustees and its chair, to divisional superintendents and field superintendents, walk this talk and stay the course in modeling these four beliefs, even when things are chaotic in their schools.

2. Embedded literacy coaches. Often allocated from within existing elementary and secondary staffing allocations (when budgets are tight, as they were in YRDSB), these are staff members who work alongside classroom teachers during the school day, demonstrating successful literacy practices in classrooms. Although they have only one-quarter to one-half of their day allocated to literacy, these classroom teachers who are literacy experts across the grades also teach in their own classrooms the rest of the day, as respected and respectful teachers who invite staff members into their classrooms to watch them teach. This is a very cost-effective model. Literacy coaches model assessment literacy that drives differentiated instruction. It is critical that these coaches are selected wisely on the basis of being exemplary teachers who are respected by their peers as knowledgeable, approachable, and supportive. These ongoing literacy learners attend and often lead district PL with curriculum consultants monthly.

3. Time-tabled literacy block. At least 100 uninterrupted minutes daily must be allocated to focused time on task on balanced literacy assessment and instruction, and at least 60 minutes for mathematical literacy. No distractions or interruptions, such as announcements, field trips, or assemblies, can occur during this dedicated literacy time. And the time tables for the one-quarter to one-half day allocated time for literacy coaches must align with the literacy block so that these teachers can get into classrooms to plan and coteach (see Chapter 4). At the secondary level, the focus is on the development of formative assessments and strong literacy instructional practices in and across all subject disciplines, emphasizing the language of each discipline (L. Sharratt & M. Sharratt, 2006). Importantly, the partial literacy coach allocation allows for these coaches to not only demonstrate new practices alongside classroom teachers but also have colleagues in their classrooms to observe them while teaching.

4. Principal leadership. Principals' deep structural under-standing of successful literacy practices in classrooms is key. Therefore, principals must be committed to attending all district literacy PL sessions with their literacy leadership teams as lead-learners. PL is mandated for field superintendents and principals to attend—not simply to be seen, but to participate as "knowledgeable others" with their school teams. Superintendents and senior leaders model focusing on data to improve student achievement and staying the course by maintaining, reviewing, and monitoring school literacy plans. There must also be modeling of these district PL sessions by principals and teacher leadership teams back at their own staff meetings.

5. Early and ongoing intervention. Reading Recovery is a highly successful program that is an excellent example of what we mean by early intervention. The program identifies the lowest-achieving children in every Grade 1 class and provides balanced intervention, with parental support, to move these lowest achievers to read and write at the expected level so that they are able to benefit from good classroom instruction. It is critical to establish ongoing intervention programs and strategies at every grade level if we really believe that all students can learn and will come to that learning at different times. Equally important, the positive consequences of early and ongoing intervention raise learners' capacity in every classroom and transfer best practice modeled in Reading Recovery training programs to classroom teachers, making this a cost-effective model and making teachers' jobs more satisfying. It ensures the increase of overall achievement levels of all students.

6. Case management approach. This approach is used to effectively review and use data to drive differentiated instruction and the selection of resources. Inclusive case management meetings during the school day bring together classroom teachers (freed up by teachers without classrooms, by vice principals, or by creative time-tabling), special education teachers, administrators, and specialist staff to scrutinize data displayed on data walls or in tracking folders (showing where all students are sequenced in the learning continuum). Discussion of student work in a case-by-case approach enables participants at the meeting to put individual faces on data. Teachers can then discuss together what instructional support is needed and how to provide it. This ensures that all teachers in the school have collective responsibility to "own" all students' achievement.

7. Literacy professional development at school staff meetings. Principals are committed to literacy professional development at staff meetings and model its importance by reducing operational items to memo format. Teachers work together to understand assessment literacy and solid instructional approaches through the literacy lens based on each school's data. This job-embedded learning ensures accountability and responsibility for all students through distributed teacher leadership.

8. In-school grade/subject meetings. These weekly after-school meetings, by division or department, focus on individual student's literacy achievement by using common assessment tools and exemplars so that same-grade/course teachers can come to common understandings of the expected standards of student work across a grade level or subject area. This collaborative examination of student work by administrators and teachers promotes consistency, ideally across classes within and across schools in a district, ultimately eliminating variation in instruction among classrooms—our goal and often parents' dismay. These meetings also provide a forum where teachers can learn and share new assessment and instructional approaches and develop a common language together.

9. Book rooms with leveled books and resources. Principals and literacy teams establish book rooms at primary, junior, intermediate, and secondary levels, where literacy coaches place leveled books and multidimensional resources for classroom teachers to use in bringing all students to the next reading level with fluency and comprehension. At the secondary level, departmental teams establish collections of multilevel resources, including multiple copies of selections of longer texts and genres such as comics, graphic text, newspapers, and magazine articles that relate specifically to a subject area of study.

10. Allocation of district and school budgets for literacy learning and resources. Publicly elected officials (trustees), senior district administrators, school administrators, and literacy leadership teams agree to allocate funding for literacy resources and continue to fund them through tough economic times. These resources, for use with students and with teacher study groups, are often recommended by district curriculum consultants at literacy content PL sessions. District program consultants support students' learning needs and teachers' professional development needs with consideration for human and materials resources, focusing on equity of outcomes for all students and learning for all teachers.

11. Action research focused on literacy. Using multiple data sources related to the school, school literacy teams work with the whole staff to develop a focused question concerning literacy and student achievement. Involving the whole staff, they collaboratively explore the answers to their action research (AR) question throughout the school year. For example, in YRDSB, the district's curriculum department offers a $1,000 grant per school for release time for occasional teachers to provide teachers on-site time to consolidate AR results. Annual school reports on the findings of these research studies are compiled into a district report to ensure that the learning is shared across schools and at the district level.

12. Parental involvement. School literacy teams work toward establishing community-home-school relationships. Many teams establish preschool literacy programs throughout the community, with teachers and consultants traveling to community centers and housing projects to run literacy hours and summer preschool–K literacy programs that model for parents how to read to kids at home as part of thoughtfully crafted school readiness programs (M. Sharratt, 2004). It is imperative that parents, students' first teachers, become our valuable resources as literacy partners at all grade levels and not just in primary school.

13. Cross-curricular literacy connections. All administrators and teachers, at all levels, find time to discuss and demonstrate to each other what cross-curricular literacy looks like in classroom practice. Then they work together to implement the teaching of literacy—and the language of the disciplines—in the content areas across all grades and subject areas. Cross-curricular connections must be valued and utilized in support of literacy instruction at all grade levels, elementary and secondary.

These 13 parameters serve as a guide to systematic action, but they play themselves out dynamically in all schools. Throughout this book, you will find vignettes demonstrating what we mean. For example, the following vignette about Thea shows how some of the parameters cluster in action (in this case, Parameters 2, 3, and 11). The parameters simultaneously serve as a planning framework, a means of dynamic implementation (as in the vignettes), and review tools to assess the presence and quality of all the components.

Vignette: Thea's Open-Door Policy (Parameters 2, 3, and 11 in Action)

"Let's talk about why we're here," Barb and Gale said to Taylor, their principal, as they entered Thea's Grade 5 demonstration classroom during the literacy block. Taylor stated emphatically that they were checking out how Thea manages her reading groups and the rest of the class at the same time. Soon they were all immersed in observing purposeful activity as the students engaged in independent reading and reflecting on their reading in their "reading response journals."

Over in one corner, Thea was working with a guided reading group. The students listened carefully to her questions about one section of the text: "What would this be like if it were you? Why do you think the author wrote that? What is her message? What evidence do you see in the text to support your answer?"

Barb and Gale were amazed at the level of questioning in the guided reading group, with the students discussing the text and asking more questions of each other as the conversation became livelier. They also noticed the focused and accountable talk by the rest of the students in class as they worked independently or in small, carefully selected groups. Barb and Gale were excited to get back to their school to put some missing literacy pieces in place and were encouraged by the insights that Taylor and Thea had provided them in their follow-up dialogue. Now they quickly had to determine today how to do it tomorrow!

As you can see from this vignette, the 13 parameters present a focus for going more deeply. Most districts underinvest in capacity building or engage in a flurry of ad hoc, unfocused activity that passes for capacity building. In our model, the 13

> I am as comfortable in York Region's Theory of Action [these 13 parameters that define the LC work] as I am in my Levis at home.
>
> (Richard Elmore, OECD Conference, UK, 2006)

parameters must be intentionally reviewed and assessed to ensure that capacity-building activities strategically align to allow for full implementation of the parameters. The goal is relentless, consistent practice across all classrooms. Reducing the variation among classroom practice is essential if we believe that all students can and will learn (Planche, Sharratt, & Belchetz, 2008).

Our successful experience in YRDSB is entirely congruent with the main findings in a recent major study of nine states, 43 district, and 180 schools conducted by Kenneth Leithwood and colleagues (2009). For example, they found that one of the most powerful sources of district influence on schools and students was the development of school leaders' collective sense of efficacy about their jobs. Our vignettes show how this efficacy stems from a clearly stated shared vision/belief and from implementing all the parameters in concert. And the following conclusion from the study could be inserted into any report about YRDSB with full accuracy:

Districts contribute most powerfully to principals' sense of efficacy by

- establishing clear purposes which become widely shared;
- unambiguously awarding priority to the improvement of instruction;
- providing flexible, varied, meaningful, and just-in-time professional development for both school administrators and their staffs;
- creating productive working relationships with all the major stakeholders;
- assisting schools in the collection, interpretation, and use of data for decision making. (Leithwood et al., 2009, p. 84)

Thus the nitty-gritty of capacity building in YRDSB resembles what basic research tells us about effective practices. In the next three chapters, we delve more deeply into how the 13 parameters work in practice in YRDSB. Then in Chapter 6 we discover that indeed there is a 14th parameter. Read on!

CHAPTER THREE

The Road to Realization

The road to realization—every teacher and every student engaged and benefiting—is essentially a sequence of scaffolding the capacity building stages. *Scaffolding* refers to supported progressive learning during which knowledge is built up. New knowledge is brought into play and connected with prior knowledge. Each layer is built on a solid foundation created by previous learnings, gradually releasing responsibility for the learning from leader to learner. With this in mind, a powerful model for moving from capacity building to realization begins with a layer of modeled practice, then adds shared practice, followed by guided practice, until the learning is self-actualized in interdependent practice. In this chapter, we take up the first three components, moving to interdependent practice in Chapter 4.

We believe this scaffolded learning model is transferable to establishing learning needed at all levels and in all contexts: districts, schools, and classrooms. Moreover, this progressive learning model results in the sustainability of increased student achievement for all—realization. Here we define briefly each of the four stages and then go on to provide more detail about each stage.

1. **Modeled practice,** the first level, initiates the capacity-building stage. Thinking big and starting small, the curriculum superintendent (Sharratt), along with a small core of strong curriculum consultants, models the components of the literacy priority, articulating how the priority was formed and why it is held with unwavering passion. Learners listen attentively and then reflect on where this fits with their current thinking, knowing, and doing.

Determining how to scaffold this new, unfamiliar information onto existing learned concepts is an important step for leaders to take.

2.   **Shared practice** continues the capacity building by inviting learners to participate in their own learning through dialogue and questioning in safe and supportive learning environments. It offers leader-led and -shaped learning that allows for collegiality, risk taking, and hence safe debate by learners. Leaders must consider how to scaffold this sharing to help all learners reach the next level of sophisticated learning.

3.   **Guided practice** is the critical transition practice that allows smooth passage of information among learners and deepens understanding from capacity building to become interdependent practice, or realization. It allows leaders to pull back and the learners to step forward, doing most of the work in thinking how to apply what has been shared. As the concept is not new anymore, there is constant "trying it out" and "talking it out" by learners while walking alongside their leaders. Leaders, as colearners with teachers, are in their schools and classrooms to practice.

4.   **Interdependent practice** is the ultimate practice, the target for which we have been aiming. Literature that deals with teaching students often refers to this as *independent practice,* but we have renamed it *interdependent practice* to ensure that our message is clear: each system/school/classroom must be tightly coupled, aligned, and not separated at any time from the central focus, purpose, or shared vision. This learner-led strategy is critical to sustainability. The organization collectively becomes as interdependent as the learners within it and approaches or surpasses the 30,000 hours required to become collectively "good" (p. 12).

Interdependent practice occurs when learners have consolidated their learning and can do it alone, with the leader continuing to offer minimal support. Importantly, the learning to reach this level has been carefully scaffolded. By definition, scaffolded learning is built layer by connecting layer—a process that is "not so fast" and results in broad-based shared experiences from the ground up (think about the discussion in Chapter 1 of the lessons from San Diego and Duval County). Finally, it should be noted that leaders can come from many different sources—literacy coaches, principals, curriculum consultants, teachers, superintendents.

But how does our progressive learning model work in practice over time? Let's examine the four stages in greater detail.

MODELED PRACTICE AT EVERY LEVEL

There is more to getting large-scale reform right than meets the eye. Our experiences show that early improvement gains can be seen to accomplish a great deal in a short period of time. But this early achievement, while critically important, cannot be overvalued as it only represents the beginning of a much deeper journey that leads to sustainable achievement levels. Modeled practice must be evident at every level in a system to promote clarity of purpose, to highlight determined singularity of focus, and to signal compelling urgency.

As the 13 parameters evolve in practice, district and school leaders individually, and in partnership, can and do model what it looks like to use and integrate the parameters to increase capacity building. They host and present at learning sessions for school leadership teams (consisting of principals, literacy coaches, special education resource teachers, department heads, and literacy leads) and are able to knowledgeably demonstrate what assessment that drives differentiated instruction looks like at every level—elementary and secondary. District leaders and curriculum consultants model the expectation that school teams, including principals as lead-learners, must attend all sessions and return to their schools to replicate the learning sessions for staff.

In modeling practice, district leaders and field superintendents regularly spend time in schools to clearly articulate not only common language but also how to move forward together. Districts leaders are diligent in modeling (1) the removal of operational barriers to the priority; (2) how to provide balanced daily elementary time tables to ensure 100-minute literacy blocks and 60-minute mathematical literacy blocks; (3) dialogue-enhancing common preparation time for same-grade or same-course teachers; and (4) increased and consistent time on instructional tasks for all students across all schools.

In schools that perform effectively, administrators are often heard articulating to staff and parents why staff members are doing what they are doing, using student performance assessment data to substantiate the why and how of their teaching strategies. Because they truly understand the focus and are committed to student achievement, administrators model by walking the talk. They are willing and able to talk about and demonstrate for staff the how of instruction that increases students' achievement.

This model necessitates that principals must be in their schools every day. They must be visible in classrooms daily, teach lessons, and allocate funds to needed teacher and student

> One principal reinforced the importance of the district's strong, consistent, and very explicit vision, stating, "Being able to say that literacy is the top priority provides me with lots of strength and power in what I say and what the school priority is, and how teachers follow it."
>
> (M. Sharratt, 2004, p. 105)

resources that support literacy learning. They must feel and be able to project to teachers that their professional success is measured by all students' achievement in their schools. Administrators and school literacy leadership teams work diligently together to recognize and remove cultural and operational obstacles to staff members learning together.

At the classroom level, teachers model high expectations and set clearly displayed performance targets for all students. They can precisely articulate the why and how of their instructional practices that often differ for each student or small groups of students. They craft instruction based on individual assessments, make flexible and fluid groupings of students, and select resources to meet diverse student needs. There are no "canned" solutions for student learning, only skillfully crafted assessment and instruction that comes from teachers having extensive instructional repertoires of high-yield strategies from which to choose the most appropriate approach needed at any given moment. These teachers, their assistants, and classroom volunteers are truly professionals, modeling that only the best output from every student is acceptable.

After years of experience, we have found that teachers who frequently model reading (using nonfiction texts) and writing (using authentic situations and relevant topics) find a magic formula to consolidate students' literacy learning—even for the most struggling students, whether girls or boys.

> To me as an elementary principal, the key is a combination of structured lessons and authentic reading and writing experiences, and I would say that must occur from kindergarten all the way up through Grade 8. I try to model that by writing back to students when they bring stuff for me to read.
>
> (quoted in M. Sharratt, 2004, p. 62)

Through modeled practice, teachers create joyful learning environments that are rich with accountable and engaging talk for students whose personal interests and aptitudes range widely. Not only in reading and writing but in every lesson, teachers are highly successful when they model new concepts taught in a variety of ways, including think-alouds, manipulatives, and making real-world connections. Most often, teachers need opportunities to see other teachers modeling these new practices in order to expand their own repertoires.

Finally, leaders at every level model learning, not just teaching. Learning is the common thread that is critical for students, teachers, principals, support staff, district leaders, and parents to model. District and school leaders model actions that build capacity across schools and systems. Teachers model actions that build school and individual learning capacity. Leaders (whether they be principals; teachers; or divisional, department, or curriculum leads) know how to manage a broad range of good ideas and turn them into focused instructional practices that increase student learning.

Shared Practice at Every Level

Scaffolding learning from leader-led modeled practice to shared practice means engaging learners as active participants. As with modeled practice, shared practice occurs outside the school itself, usually in a central location to bring together district, school, and classroom leaders to share the learning in a safe and supportive environment that lets them take risks confidently. It takes thoughtful, structured planning to scaffold this new learning onto modeled practice.

District inservice sessions and smaller networked learning communities are established to share learning with school leadership teams; the expectation is that they will plan how to transfer knowledge and skills, and create cultures of learning back at their schools. At these sessions, superintendents and district program staff, as knowledgeable others, share beliefs and related experiences about how to increase students' literacy achievement. Beginning each session with student assessment data, they build understanding of how assessment must inform instruction for each and every student. In return for this shared practice support, superintendents expect to see evidence of initial improvement of student learning in every school for all students within a defined time period.

As Kathy Soule points out, conversations with operational, plant, and planning superintendents and managers must occur to ensure that appropriate structures are in place to provide optimum literacy learning conditions. Discussions must include scrutiny of school sites for cleanliness; items in disrepair; nonfunctional technology; and well-marked, safe play areas. If structure drives behavior, then planning for the addition of smaller rooms for more focused, small-group instruction and places for centralized, shared resources, such as book rooms, are key factors in producing positive learning behaviors.

Another critical shared practice is the districts' plan for involvement of school councils, trustees, parent-teacher associations, and all other advisory stakeholder groups in improvement planning, ensuring that these stakeholders are on focus with the priority and can, from their own contexts, begin to articulate what the priority means to them. Similarly, a powerful, honest local media strategy will train the media to read the priority, understand its outcomes, and see how to accurately and sensitively report on them.

At the school level, shared practice involves administrators and leadership teams sharing beliefs, experiences, and an understanding of assessment practices and high-yield instructional strategies with all staff at regularly scheduled professional activity days, staff meetings, and parent

We have a senior team structure that is inclusive. We are a small district, and each week the full senior team, including Information Services, Facility Services, Business Services, etc., come together with our system principal leaders to discuss system priorities. All decisions begin with looking at the impact on student learning and the implementation of the literacy agenda. All department planning meetings have cross-departmental reps . . . always someone from literacy and student success. We include a component of literacy/student success in most board and trustee committee meetings. It is my belief that this "system saturation" will lead to a "habit of mind" for system and school leaders, including those in leadership positions in schools, union groups, and school councils.

(Kathy Soule, Director of Education [CEO], Hastings and Prince Edward District School Board, personal communication, September 2008).

There must be a process in place to continually acknowledge and address system/operational barriers that arise and allow for the ability to adjust in order to ensure that student learning is the priority. For this to happen, districts must have the flexibility to schedule and accommodate students in ways that are different from what have been our traditional structures.

(Gale Harild, Curriculum Administrator, York Region District School Board, personal communication, September 2008)

nights, often using a variety of online interactive technologies. Nights to share student achievement (e.g., curriculum nights, literacy nights, arts performances, family math nights, town hall meetings, festivals, and student-led conferences) engage and inspire parents and the community to become active participants in the schools' safe and supportive learning environments. Inviting local media to these celebrations is a powerful way to share students' achievement with the broader community.

In shared practice, school administrators know what precise, intentional assessment and instructional practice look like in classrooms. They are visible in classrooms and accessible to discuss student learning with teachers at any time. Professional learning (PL) sessions include the use of video clips of successful practice in areas that student data indicate are areas of needed teacher learning. Shared viewing promotes dialogue and a willingness to try new classroom practices with others, and it pushes forward what is possible and necessary to consider in all classrooms.

School improvement plans are developed as a shared process and reflect the literacy priority as being integral to every part of the plan. In this way, all school improvement plans align with the district improvement plan, which reflects the provincial/state priority to promote all students' literacy improvement. Based on school data and aligned with the priority, the school budget is openly developed and shared with staff and parents. This transparent decision making allows for input, adjustment, and ownership through open discussion.

In shared practice, teachers have access to current and inclusive resources at varied levels of difficulty in order to meet a wide range of learner needs. Time tables are built so that teachers have common preparation periods to plan with each other and scheduled time to work with same-grade or same-course teachers and to visit in each other's classrooms to learn from one another. Common planning time gives teachers opportunities to discuss and reflect, which leads to changed classroom practices.

At the classroom level, teachers move from modeling learning expectations for students to sharing the learning with students by inviting their active participation in the lessons and in developing assessments and rubrics. Teachers use effective group work techniques to build in individual accountability as well as group performance norms. They observe students daily as part of their ongoing assessment and share next steps with them, using timely descriptive feedback, thereby making explicit for students the necessary literacy skills that are often only implied in curriculum expectations. Teachers use shared writing, a powerful technique at every level, to actively involve students in their learning to read and reading to learn. After all, knowing how to write is powerful evidence of knowing how to read.

In every lesson, teachers share academic and social/emotional goals with students and evaluate them with students at the end of the lesson. By using inclusion activities, teachers establish a community of shared learning and caring as well as a group of cared-for learners. When teachers spend time with each other, gathering and sharing resources that are appropriate, relevant, and engaging for their students, it necessitates that they know their students' interests and needs.

A most important way that teachers can share their successful practice is by opening their classroom doors and inviting others in so that they can learn from each other. We see in this the movement from a "we-they" cultural orientation to a "we-we" commitment. Classroom teachers begin to identify with "my school," not just "my classroom." School staff develop commitments to "my district," not just "my school." Teachers who work with knowledgeable and deeply involved administrators feel compelled to invite them into their classrooms to work with them and witness their changed practices. In this way, they share and celebrate their collaborative work to increase student achievement. One such committed principal, a true instructional leader, aptly explained it this way:

> When teachers realized that they didn't have to solve problems alone and that every student was important, they then understood that every student belonged to every teacher and administrator, not just to them alone. It was then that they opened their classroom doors. (M. Sharratt, 2004, pp. 114–115)

In other words, when teachers feel that they are not alone, but working together with a common purpose and shared

I am a teacher. Every day I face over 30 Grade 6 students in an economically challenged area, and I desperately need to believe that I am not in this alone—I need to *know* that the work I am doing is accountable, research-based, data-driven, reflective, and responsive to the needs of each learner's future. Furthermore, and perhaps more important, I need to *feel* that I am making a difference and that my "contextual accountability" is valid and can be *understood* and *supported* by all stakeholders.

(Pamela Crawford, Bracebridge Public School, Trillium Lakelands District School Board, personal communication, September 2008)

practice, a cultural shift occurs. This is the essence of moving beyond modeled practice to embrace shared practice at every level.

Finding time to visit classrooms and creating opportunities to discuss what was seen are invaluable administrator pursuits. When there is a commitment at the school and district levels to sharing practice, leaders find the time to support such mutual learning.

GUIDED PRACTICE AT EVERY LEVEL

Modeling and sharing are not sufficient. Everyone in the system needs to get better and better at instructional practice, and in the process take more and more ownership over increasingly precise capacity-building activities. We call this guided practice.

Guided practice is a change in the learning and leading balance. Learners step forward, taking greater control of their learning. Leaders step back, releasing the leadership reins, which is somewhat hard for some, but necessary for all. Now we move beyond the initial modeling of capacity building, and beyond pullout shared practice learning sessions, to a deeper experience with teachers and administrators, embedding assessment and instructional literacy in classrooms for each student. The school-based work in this stage requires much more precision, focus, and alignment than we or others previously thought.

In our earlier research, we found that it is not the surface beliefs and understandings that make a difference but rather the deep understanding and commitment, staying the course, and detailed knowhow that comes from learning by doing and reflecting on practice (L. Sharratt & Fullan, 2006). This is what allows leaders and learners to graduate to guided practice, the stage in which we get learners to do more. This stage involves a more fine-grained analysis of what has to happen in every school, in every class, so that the differentiation of instruction is the norm at all levels.

Guided practice fosters development of strategies that enable teachers and leaders to learn more about how to precisely engage in continuous improvement of classroom practice. Leaders are able to conceptualize and carry out their roles with ever-increasing knowledge, commitment, and precision. The gradual release of responsibility from districts to schools, from schools to classrooms, and from teachers to students has been carefully planned and scaffolded to become observable at this stage. At every level—district, school, and classroom—everyone is walking the talk and talking the walk about how to increase student achievement.

In guided practice, policy and funding come together to underscore that there is one student body to be dealt with—not students in regular education and students in special education. Hard work, strong will, and perseverance to break down existing structural and funding barriers are required to reach a common understanding that effective teaching and learning that makes a difference is necessary for all students and there is not a different or exclusionary professional practice for some only.

In the District

This guided practice starts with the disaggregation of data to determine the lowest performing or "stuck" schools in order to differentiate support. The district not only identifies these schools but differentiates the support to

In a keynote address at the York Region District School Board's Quest for Literacy and Leadership Conference, November 2003, Sir Michael Barber captured the essence of what guided practice looks like for leaders at every level:

> The leaders' job—at every level—is to commit to the priority, to create the urgency, to back best practice and then, in the time lag between implementation and results, to hold their nerve. That's what is necessary in your country at the provincial level, school board level, school level, and indeed classroom level—keeping the faith. Leaders can demonstrate their leadership in literacy in all kinds of ways, but one thing I would stress is this: if you're running a school system—when you meet someone from the school system, after you say, "How are you?" you should ask, "How's your literacy program?" "What are your results like in literacy?" So, every single question is about literacy.

them in terms of instructional support to the teachers and leaders. In York Region District School Board (YRDSB), these *intensive support schools* are supported by guided practice until steady improvement is shown, which takes longer for some schools than others. The important point here is that all school superintendents and district leaders agree on the performance data used to select schools that will receive this additional support from curriculum consultants who, as knowledgeable others, walk alongside administrators and teacher leaders in the schools. Superintendents, administrators, and teachers recognize that this is equity—differentiating resource support by need—not an example of equality, whereby all schools receive resource allocations that are divided equally among them, whether they have differing needs or not. Our experience tells us that if district, school, and teacher leaders embrace our definition of equity, then they are ready to embrace the notion of all schools and all students being supported differently to increase student achievement. One size does not fit all. This is walking the talk of guided practice.

Putting additional resources and time for support from curriculum consultants in data-identified intensive support schools is of immeasurable value in increasing the efficacy of all teachers and administrators in those schools. Reciprocally, this experience also enhances the learning of the curriculum staff so that they become even more intentional and focused on instruction that addresses the needs of every student. Every second or third year, the system data used in the selection of these schools must be updated and reviewed. In most cases, the intensively supported schools' results have improved because of new learning by their staff members and leadership so that the support can then be moved on to a new set of schools. Thus there must be a carefully crafted transitioning of schools moving on from the support and those moving into the support. (See the Chapter 5 story on Crosby Heights, a school where this is happening.)

During sessions with small clusters of schools, superintendents and curriculum/program staff, as knowledgeable others, come together to guide practice in identifying formative assessment tools and to demonstrate the effective use of daily and ongoing formative assessment in every classroom. There are no hierarchical lines about learners here. Everyone contributes to moving the concept of formative assessment (assessment today that becomes instruction tomorrow) from a cursory understanding to a deep, structured understanding in every school. To assist in this guided practice, staffing made available from the district is used to ensure that thoughtfully selected literacy coaches in all schools have partial time during the school day to work alongside administrators and teachers. When literacy coaches advise; assist, model, and guide instruction; and then give constructive feedback, they show that they are credible, build deeper understandings, and promote trust with their colleagues. Selection of literacy coaches is key here; positions are filled by knowledgeable, respected, and respectful teachers.

To guide practice further, teachers and administrators must have opportunities to observe and discuss successful practice in classrooms, such as those of master teachers, literacy coaches, tutors, divisional leads, or department heads. In YRDSB, demonstration classrooms are available, if not at every grade level, at least at every division level. Administrators creatively find ways to free up one or two classroom teachers at a time so that they can visit together to see what effective practice is (including the seamless integration of technology as a powerful instructional tool to engage students) and have time to discuss what they have seen and how it applies to changing practice given their own contexts. In YRDSB this demonstration class strategy is known as Literacy@School, one of 12 school sites worldwide that are recognized and rewarded in the Microsoft Innovative Schools Project.

> As a literacy coach, I was able, in my role, to go into classrooms and work with teachers. First of all, I started by supporting them while they were doing assessment with their students, and then working with them, either team teaching or modeling a certain strategy within their classrooms. I developed lessons with these teachers, and also on my own, and went into their classrooms with them observing me to begin.
>
> (quoted in M. Sharratt, 2004, p. 68)

We know that districts must radically reconsider and remove school structures that get in the way of educators having time to visit and learn from one another. For example, time tables must allow not only scheduled time for classroom teachers to learn with literacy coaches, but also time to come together in a case management approach (Parameter 6; see Chapter 2) in order to scrutinize student data and focus on all teachers and administrators being responsible for the improvement of all students, not just the ones in "my class." Special education structures meld with regular education structures to honor the focus on all students. Bringing together regular and special education departments takes energy, will, and perseverance to break down established hierarchical and layered structures, but this is necessary so that we can focus on the impactful instruction we are advocating—for *all* students.

Training needs to be carefully guided in order to maximize critical thinking and effective action. What are the high-yield, guided training experiences that give learners and leaders the knowledge and engagement they need to reach interdependent practice, or realization? We suggest three powerful training models at the district level that guide practice and lead to realization: Reading Recovery, action research, and literacy walks. Specialized, in-depth Reading Recovery training enables classroom teachers to learn the theory and practice how to teach the lowest-performing Grade 1 students how to read "at level" within a period of 12 to 20 weeks. Training for action

research and literacy walks involves school teams, including principals and superintendents, learning together.

Reading Recovery Training

Reading Recovery aims to prevent early reading difficulties that
often permanently derail student improvement. This exemplary
training model directly addresses Parameter 5: early and ongoing
intervention is critical. Reading Recovery is a bridge between classroom teaching on the one hand and special needs provisions on the
other. It is designed to be proactive and preventative.

After the intervention, many children no longer need Reading
Recovery support and are able to profit from good first teaching
instruction provided by the regular Grade 1 classroom teacher.
Teachers find that there is an increase in the achievement of all
students because they are learning from a higher common point of
departure. Reading Recovery is a powerful catalyst for change in
both student learning and teacher efficacy. It is cost-effective when
trained teachers are able to utilize their skills in the remaining half
of their teaching assignments (as Reading Recovery takes up half
of their time), share their practice with colleagues, and cycle into
full-time classroom teaching
after four or five years, allowing
the opportunity for others to
be trained. Real achievement
gains are made when Reading
Recovery–trained teachers move
on to become junior or intermediate teachers as the same skill
sets are critical in these divi-
sions, too. Strong teachers recognize that the same skills needed for
teaching reading in Grade 1 apply to older students still struggling to
comprehend.

> Dr. Marie Clay, creator of Reading
> Recovery, said, "We must design
> the best available lessons for the
> hardest-to-teach children as early
> as possible."
>
> (quoted in Clay, 2005, p. 17)

Over the past 10 years, in YRDSB there has been a determined
and collective effort to reach and sustain full implementation of
Reading Recovery so that all students can meet the provincial standards in reading and writing (YRDSB, 2003–2004). As a result,
standards have been met in every category. Reading Recovery creates important cost benefits for school districts by reducing the need
to spend money for potentially unnecessary assessments and/or
interventions. Intensive, individual diagnostic teaching of students

can often reduce unnecessary referrals and special identification of students. YRDSB's CEO, Bill Hogarth, and trustee chair, Bill Crothers, went on record long ago declaring that they would protect Reading Recovery from union strife—it was non-negotiable. This is a bold example of not only believing that all

> I think having Reading Recovery training is a huge tool for me. The two Reading Recovery teachers in our school are both very highly respected and are always an excellent source of knowledge for all our teachers who are looking to improve their literacy programs.
>
> (quoted in M. Sharratt, 2004, p. 86)

students can learn but also ensuring that teachers have the skills taught in Reading Recovery to make it happen.

In this stage of guided practice, the impossible becomes the possible. That is to say, we utilize the strengths of the Reading Recovery training model (in particular, the behind-the-glass teaching model and resulting "critical friend" feedback) as an integral strategy to develop shared beliefs, understandings, and teaching expertise across district departments.

It is important to let achievement data tell the story of instruction that works, like Reading Recovery, in order to build one strong instructional team across regular and special education. This will ensure rigor in the use of data and provide all teachers with a deep understanding of how to use daily assessment to teach reading, writing, and mathematical literacy to struggling early learners.

No other early intervention reading model gets the results or has the evidence to support it that Reading Recovery does. (See also *The Long-Term Costs of Literacy Difficulties,* 2006; What Works Clearinghouse, 2007). Finally, like all of the key components in our model, no one component stands alone; Reading Recovery works successfully because it is fully implemented and operates in concert with the other 12 parameters.

Action Research Training

In YRDSB, action research is based on school data and is collaboratively designed by all staff focusing on a question meant to cause reflection on practice and an examination of how to increase student achievement. This is not the traditional definition of action research; in fact, Kurt Lewin, who first proposed the concept in 1967, clearly identified that action research should bear scientific characteristics (Ostinelli, 2008). What is important in our iteration of

There is a culture of research and reflective practice at all levels of the organization:

- Students, teachers, schools, districts, and communities work closely with researchers to continuously learn and improve.
- Teachers and principals feel comfortable using research to learn about, assess, and reflect on their own teaching practice.
- Broader school communities are actively engaged in the research process, feel comfortable bringing forward research issues, and appreciate the role of research in improving practice.
- Research is seen as fundamental to learning and change... in particular, action research... involving ongoing reflective practice.

(Colleen Stanton and Bob Harper, personal communication, September 2008)

action research is that not only are data used, but data are produced in a whole-school collaborative approach to inquiry. Data on student achievement, from multiple sources, are triangulated, relentlessly scrutinized, and then used to form a focused question that the staff work on throughout the school year. Teachers and administrators then gather data from multiple sources, including district PL sessions, networking groups, book study groups, and experts' presentations on webcasts and at conferences. Collaboratively, time is spent analyzing the data to answer the focused action research question. Findings are written up to inform professional learning sessions needed for school staff and across the district, next steps in school plans for continuous improvement, and annual improvement reports (see Chapter 6) submitted to the district and presented to superintendents, parents, and students.

Literacy Walk Training

Literacy walk training is our third example of core training that guides practice toward realization. YRDSB has developed its own model of walking in classrooms as a way of strengthening knowledge of what we see in them. The program trains superintendents, administrators, and curriculum staff to walk into classrooms briefly to look for specifics in literacy, assessment, and instructional practice; note safe and supportive learning environments; and focus on students' thinking. Training includes practice in developing reflective, nonthreatening questions to pose to classroom teachers, after many visits, to engage them in dialogue about and reflections on their practice.

As Ryan (2003) states, "particularly effective are dialogues that encourage teachers to become aware of, and critically reflect on, their learning and professional practice" (p. 182). This nonevaluative approach takes time to move to a higher level of questioning that is meant to offer a deliberate pause for practitioners who seek to improve their practice together. These questions have the potential to turn into literacy conversations when, after viewing classes to observe patterns, an administrator frames a conversation with a question that focuses on instruction. These reflective conversations are meant to engage individuals and professional communities in elaborating on, extending, applying, and evaluating their thinking to create new knowledge and to go beyond what they already know.

The purpose of a literacy walk is to create a collaborative culture with a focus on students' literacy achievement. It involves teachers talking about and sharing their decision-making process in the design of classroom practices that meet the needs of all learners (YRDSB, 2007c). Because we realized that literacy walks could be seen as merely an evaluative tool if not understood, and hence be problematic to union officials, we trained union leaders alongside a core team of superintendents, elementary and secondary principals, and curriculum consultants. During their positive, firsthand experience with the approach, we built a knowledge base together that reflected and highlighted what they came to see as the nonevaluative nature of the approach. This initial training proved invaluable in moving us forward as a system and allowing us to go deeper by designing and implementing our own literacy walks followed by coaching conversations for all staff.

Vignette: Robert Is Walking Again
(Parameters 1, 7, 10, and 11 in Action)

Robert is taking another literacy walk—the second time today, this time during the intermediate's literacy block. Careful not to interrupt the teacher or students at work, he leans down beside Jackson to ask him what he's learning today. He's writing about his group's participation in an activity they have just finished together. He talks to him about the social goal and academic goal that he is to think about. He points to his group getting ready to discuss their individual and group participation in the activity and hurries off to show them his pie chart of what the participation looked like from his viewpoint.

(Continued)

(Continued)

At the next staff meeting, Robert comments on the effective group work practices in Madeleine's classroom. By the end of the term, Robert has been able to precisely comment on the strengths of practice in all of the teachers' classrooms. Using his specific and clear observations of instruction, he builds trusting and respectful relationships with staff and heightens their awareness of his expectations of assessment literacy and intentional instruction, thus moving the staff forward in a positive way. After the staff meeting, two teachers ask Robert if they can visit Madeleine's classroom to learn more about the effective group work strategies she uses to engage all students. Robert happily arranges for coverage . . . and goes with them to learn more for himself.

In Classrooms

At the classroom level, many successful elementary and secondary teachers use the progression of modeled, shared, and guided practice in all of their teaching approaches to ensure that students experience scaffolded learning and the gradual release of responsibility to become independent learners. This is particularly true in using writing to increase students' literacy achievement in every discipline. Increased emphasis on writing, in many forms and for all kinds of purposes, may be a critical key to improving student learning. Internationally recognized literacy expert Margaret Meek (1991) does not mince words about the power and magic of writing:

> Literacy begins with writing. A mark, a scratch even, a picture or a sign made by one person which is interpreted and understood by others may be regarded as a form of writing. The idea is simple enough. Once we have grasped it, even the hieroglyphics of the Egyptians seem, if not familiar, then at least part of the same world as our word processors. To me, writing seems to be a perpetual and recurrent miracle. (p. 18)

Meek continues to use a broad view to reinforce the importance of writing:

> Those who study the history of writing are convinced that it is one of the most momentous of all human inventions. It makes possible the use of language beyond speech. It makes us conscious of

language itself in ways that affect both our public and private lives. It creates what is to read, and, therefore, readers. (p. 23)

Franklin (2003) reinforces these notions as well as Parameter 13, a focus on cross-curricular literacy:

Writing across the curriculum is defined as a tool for developing thinking. Students learn and practice writing skills in most, if not all, of their classes, from language arts to social studies and even in fact-based subjects such as earth science and mathematics. (p. 4)

We had the opportunity to watch the literacy coach from one of our highly successful schools guide practice by demonstrating writing techniques for staff members. Like many others, she and her principal believe that when students are engaged in authentic writing tasks that require higher-order and critical thinking, significant improvement is evidenced in both reading and writing scores on provincial assessments. We know we can help all students achieve success with reading through individually crafted, authentic, nonfiction writing tasks, and Allen (2003) concurs:

As a nation we can barely begin to imagine how powerful K–12 education might be if writing were put in its proper focus. Facility with writing opens students up to the pleasure of exercising their minds in ways that grinding on facts, details, and information never will. More than a way of knowing, writing is an act of discovery. (p. 1)

On this topic, Meek (1991) stresses the following:

Nowadays, we can all become writers. The tools are readily in hand; the new technologies, word processors and print shops which make our words look as good as anyone else's are user-friendly. The greatest changes in literacy are associated with writing, chiefly because the range of discourses and the means of both renewing and reinventing them have become more generally available. (p. 28)

Meek's guidance is substantiated by the results of a pilot project undertaken by the Peace River North School District in Fort St. John, British Columbia, in Canada. The district saw a 22 percent increase

Elmore (1999, in Fullan, 2003, p. 57) states that priority one is that "educational reform is about instruction and only instruction.... Instructional improvement is a long multi-stage process involving awareness, planning, implementation and reflection.... The good ideas come from talented people working together.... Collegiality, caring and respect are paramount.

in English scores after students were given laptop computers to compose, edit, and refine their writing. This Wireless Writing Program led to substantial improvements for grade school students particularly in the area of written expression (Wolchak, 2004). Similar research replicated in YRDSB positively validated these findings.

In guided practice, not only do classroom teachers focus on writing to increase students' literacy achievement, but they also find ways to refine their practice, for example, by being involved with lesson study, which was first devised in Japan (Lewis, 2002). Lesson study adds pressure and support for guiding precise, specific, and targeted assessment that drives instruction by teachers who are keenly interested in improving their practice.

Lesson study is collaborative inquiry whereby small groups of same-grade or same-course teachers come together with a curriculum expert (in the case of YRDSB, a literacy coach) and work from curriculum expectations and achievement charts to plan a lesson, create rich learning tasks for students, and then decide who will teach the lesson. During instruction, the other teachers gather in the classroom, not to watch the teacher who offered to teach, but to observe the students' thinking during the cooperatively designed lesson. At the debriefing afterwards, the teachers decide what worked, what didn't, and what they would do differently next time to foster students' higher-order thinking. Another teacher from the group volunteers to teach the revised lesson, with the fellow teachers observing again, always with a focus on students' thinking. As one YRDSB teacher said, "A fascinating process—of going from brainstorming ideas that is freely divergent thinking to firming up specific steps in a lesson. Establishing group norms to maximize participation is a valuable tool to frame this experience in a way that involved everybody." Another added his final impressions of being involved in lesson study: "It was eye-opening to follow a lesson from planning to providing the lesson. Watching without interfering gave me a chance to really understand how and what students were thinking as well as doing. The debrief after the lesson was so valuable. As a teacher, one cannot see every-thing going on. By having observers jotting notes, one learns a tremendous amount about each student during a group activity."

Kate Diakiw, principal of YRDSB's Silver Stream Public School, believes passionately in this approach:

> Lesson study has been the most powerful job-embedded PL with which I have ever been associated. It has moved the greatest number of teachers into new practices. That has a lot to do with the "constructivist method" of learning and the high degree of collaborative work—that is, teachers' thinking that influences each other's work. These teachers work together and share own-ership of ideas and strategies. They see their jointly designed plan in action and instantly see revisions that can make a difference to student achievement. When they try the lesson again, post revi-sions, they have been astounded, in many cases, to see the low-est level of achievement in the second class exceed the highest level of achievement in the first class. I have seen more teachers be "blown away" by the proof that what they do can change and increase the level of student achievement. When teachers create the knowledge themselves, it seems to be significantly more influential to changing their daily practice than any workshop or book. While those are valid and important forms of learning, some teachers spend their reading or watching time thinking: "This won't work for me in my class" or "I don't know what they mean by that" or "Why are they doing that?" All of those doubts and worries melt away in lesson study because they are in the middle of it, figuring it out and trying it out, with a team. It is awfully hard for participants to turn their backs on something they have just proven to themselves works, through their own ideas and efforts. (personal communication, April 2009)

In lesson study, teachers explore the notion of assessment that differentiates instruction in a safe and supportive environment by being attentive to student thinking, being alert to student voice, clar-ifying points of view with accountable talk, and developing a broad repertoire of instructional strategies on which to draw when devel-oping lessons collaboratively. In this way, we believe that lesson study is a powerful example of how teachers can develop their craft, guiding each other's practice to review and refine instruction.

While principals and teachers articulate good intentions about working together in dynamic and effective ways, their work also appears significantly complicated by the complexities of interpersonal relationships and the impact of working cultures. As well, trust appears a prerequisite to developing deeper forms of collaborative work.

(Planche, 2004, 2007)

In guided practice we have seen that when teachers are open to incorporating successful teaching practices that are grounded in research and experience, they develop a deep understanding of the need to focus on every students' thinking to bring them beyond their comfort zone to the next level of critical thinking.

The cultural norm is that teachers and administrators reach out passionately and resourcefully to colleagues—refining practice together and using data that are consistent and agreed upon—to move all students forward. Once the new culture of learning through modeling, sharing, and guiding reaches a critical mass, we believe that sustained system reform, or realization, will be within our grasp. In other words, as system capacity increases, intentional and focused efforts yield greater return because the whole system gets better at what it does. The extraordinary becomes possible without superhuman effort (Fullan & Sharratt, 2007). And when this happens, the synergy of continuous improvement on a large scale becomes a realization.

Thus, guided practice signals a shift in focus from what teachers and administrators need to do to what students can do, independently and consistently, across all grades, schools, and disciplines. As we discuss in the next chapter, the catalyst for the transition from guided practice to interdependent practice, or realization, is the focus on students in classrooms. District leaders, teachers, administrators, and parents see, discuss, and support the potential in all students.

Vignette: How Did Louis Get to Grade 11? (Parameters 1, 6, and 8 in Action)

Louis finally admitted to his teacher today that he couldn't read. After a long discussion, she learned that every day his dad had driven him to school, Louis tricked him into thinking that he could read. As they drove and chatted, Louis read imaginary words to his dad from his texts.

He secretly hated school, but that wasn't much of a surprise to his teachers as he was in trouble almost every day he was there. It was his second school district this year; he was banished from the first for his "incorrigible behavior." Louis found ways of acting out—trying every teacher's patience intentionally to divert their attention, he thought, from finding out.

One day, at a secondary school case management meeting, one of Louis's teachers, Stephanie, voiced the problem by bravely saying, "I think it's a reading problem, can you help?" The teachers collaboratively decided on the diagnostic assessment that Stephanie would use to determine the problem; then, after Louis confirmed his problem, Stephanie took him in every night after school with a tailor-made reading intervention program initially geared to his very low reading level *and* his interests. The case management team agreed to meet with Stephanie each week to debrief and recommend further instructional approaches if needed. Stephanie began by modeling simple texts, building vocabulary, and writing, using computer technology to reinforce the skills she taught.

After months, moving on to shared and guided practice, the words became more than a blurry jumble on the page to Louis. He began to independently read texts, with comprehension, at grade level with only minimal help from Stephanie. "Once I found his instructional starting points and corresponding novels at his level, we were off—and he could do it!"

Louis himself says, "I was so angry at everything around me—frustrated that I couldn't do the homework, read the textbooks or write—that I took it out on the teachers. I would get into trouble and get suspended every day and call my mom. Now I pick up a newspaper and instead of just looking for the Maple Leafs' scores, I can read what's happening in the world."

And Stephanie concurs, "Louis was ready and brave enough, and had lots of people cheering for him. I truly believe all students can learn, given time and the right support."

The road to realization is one of deeper and wider learning. New capacities to implement high-quality literacy programs are continually developed through modeling, sharing, and guiding practice in a joint learning proposition within and across schools, and between schools and the district. But this is not sufficient for sustainable improvement. For that you need coequal, codetermined interdependent practice.

CHAPTER FOUR

Interdependent Practice

The fourth and final stage of our model to accomplish systematic, system-wide reform is interdependent practice, or realization. Realization is a much more sophisticated, systematic approach to deepening educational reform. It requires the elements and conditions provided by successful transition through the first three stages: (a) "on the ground" expertise in every school that is precisely matched by the same expertise at the district level, (b) authentic leaders in schools and districts who understand not only successful instructional practices but also strategic timing, and (c) a collective commitment to knowing when to do the right thing and how to do the right things right in order to move a system and its schools forward. It is a focused mobilization against inertia.

Figure 4.1 shows the results of this mobilization. Trend data indicate that this model of progressive levels of learning is not only working but sustaining achievement for all students in York Region District School Board (YRDSB).

Once again, it can be said that YRDSB's effectiveness is mirrored by the findings in the major study by Leithwood and colleagues (2009). In this research in successful districts, as in YRDSB, principals did very specific and systematic things to influence practice and student learning, such as the following:

- Principal leadership plays a key role in establishing the purposes and expectations for data use, structured opportunities (collegial groups and time), data use training and assistance, access to expertise, and follow-up actions (p. 120). When

Figure 4.1 York Region District School Board Trend Data in Provincial Assessments

Education, Quality, and Accountability Office (EQAO) Assessment Results: All Participating Students at Levels 3 and 4, including ESL	1999: Baseline Year Before Districts' Literacy Focus	2008	% Increase
Grade 3 Reading	59	71	12
Grade 3 Writing	66	79	13
Grade 3 Mathematics	70	80	10
Grade 6 Reading	61	78	17
Grade 6 Writing	59	81	22
Grade 6 Mathematics	63	77	14
EQAO Results for ESL			
% ESL Learners of Total Grade 3	4%	9%	5%
% ESL Learners of Total Grade 6	4%	7%	3%
Grade 3 ESL Reading	34	66	32
Grade 3 ESL Writing	47	75	28
Grade 3 ESL Mathematics	62	77	15
Grade 6 ESL Reading	27	67	40
Grade 6 ESL Writing	27	74	47
Grade 6 ESL Mathematics	62	79	17
Ontario Secondary School Literacy Test (Grade 10: 15-year-olds, diploma-bearing assessment)	Oct. 2002, 77% pass	2008, 88% pass	11
% of Students reading at the end of Grade 1 (using PM Benchmark Assessment Tool)	59	84	25

Source: Planche & Sharratt, 2008.

principals do not attend to these specific tasks, "teachers are certainly not doing it on their own" (p. 120).

- Principal leadership is specifically and systematically developed through the preparation of potential new school leaders, developing principals on the job, and "ensuring productive leadership succession" (p. 97).

> Districts must consider their long-term plans for leadership succession and shorter-term processes for recruiting and retaining these new principals.
>
> (Belchetz, 2004, p. 290)

In these respects, the effective principals and districts studied by Leithwood and colleagues (2009), and those of YRDSB, are virtually one and the same phenomenon. As the improvement work of districts and principals progresses, instructional practice gets more precise, specific, and powerful (high yield). It goes deeper into strong instructional practice and wider in engaging all students as partners in learning. Figure 4.2 captures much of this difference in comparing guided with interdependent practice.

Will, perseverance, and trust building are necessary inputs as well as positive outcomes of realization. Figuring out what the right things are, finding out how to do them, and doing them everywhere for all students—continuously assessing and adding new strategies—is realization. This vision and moral imperative of increased student literacy achievement must be clearly evident not only in the vertical alignment throughout the system (district, schools, and classrooms), but also in the horizontal coherence created across the system (among leaders in the district, schools, and classrooms relating the same message).

> Interdependent practice is about moving from "doer" to "enabler" wherever possible, not only at the district level, but also in the schools with administrators, teachers, and parents. Enabling means ensuring that all have the tools, the resources, and the necessary modeling to carry on by themselves.
>
> (Gale Harild, Curriculum Administrator, York Region District School Board, personal communication, September 2008)

Later (in Chapter 6), we will introduce the role of the state or province. So far, we have focused on the district—in the case of YRDSB, a large system to be sure. For realization to become embedded, there needs to be coherence across what we have

Figure 4.2 Guided Versus Interdependent Practice

Guided Practice as Capacity Building (teaching a few)	Interdependence as Realization (learning for all)
Teachers' professional learning occurs more often in their schools:	**Embedded refinement of assessment and instruction occurs in all classrooms:**
Teachers develop formative assessments together.	Teachers use formative assessments in classrooms to inform instruction.
Teachers assess student work collaboratively so that assessments have the same standards across grades and courses.	Student work improves; there is no variation among assessment and instruction in same grades and courses across a district.
Teachers develop a repertoire of assessment and instructional strategies.	Teachers use a repertoire of strategies matched to students' needs identified by formative data.
Teachers develop a common language.	Teachers and students use the same appropriate common language.
The school team takes ownership of improvement.	Teachers and students take ownership of improvement.
There is a high degree of teacher buy-in (engagement).	There is a high degree of student buy-in (engagement).
Teachers voice openness to incorporating best teaching practices grounded in research in order to improve student achievement.	Students' voice is heard in classrooms more than teachers' voice.
Teachers develop a deep understanding of curriculum expectations/learning intentions and post them and the criteria for success in classrooms for students to see.	Students develop an improved understanding of learning expectations and can articulate them and develop with teachers what they must do to reach them.
Teachers develop an understanding of achievement charts and how to construct rich tasks based on the achievement chart categories.	Students receive meaningful, timely, descriptive feedback and can clearly articulate what they need to do to improve.
Teachers develop and effectively use common assessments and mark students' work collaboratively to reach consensus.	Students self-assess and set goals from explicit feedback received.
Teachers understand how to use assessment data to plan for differentiated instruction.	Student learning is based on strengths and needs; students know how to learn and can express it (metacognition).

You know that you've reached realization when you're getting greater results—more impact in terms of student learning—than the same amount of effort that you're putting into it.

(Robyn Welch, Student Achievement Officer, Ontario Literacy and Numeracy Secretariat, personal communication, September 2008)

called *tri-level reform:* the district, school, and community. YRDSB began its journey in 1999, four years before the government got in the act with a parallel deliberate strategy based on the same premises.

Realization is what happens when excellence and equity in teaching and learning are embedded in policy legislation that not only ensures increased students' literacy achievement is an expectation but also is a way of wisely advancing our greatest resource—our children.

The following depiction may sound idealistic except that by the time you get to the interdependent stage, you will have transformed yourself, your district, and your school such that, "suddenly," it is not far-fetched. It is indeed the logical outcome in the positive progression. Momentum builds as all teachers' knowledge increases and focuses on all students achieving high proficiency.

INTERDEPENDENT PRACTICE AT THE DISTRICT LEVEL

Full implementation occurs when all departments plan together and budget lines become "our resources" to be used to ensure increased student learning, when community is part of the school and sees the school as a resource for itself as well as for its children.

(Hazel Dick, Curriculum Administrator, Reading Recovery Program, York Region District School Board, personal communication, August 2008)

At the district level, then, realization is achieved when both human and material resources that are spent on assessment and instruction are never in jeopardy, even in tough economic times.

Data providing evidence of improvement is delivered electronically to administrator, teacher, and parent desktops in a timely way, making results transparent. There is consensus on achievement standards, what they look and sound like in classrooms. Stuck and declining schools are a thing of the past as district and school staff and parents begin every conversation with comments that focus on student improvement. All understand the serious commitment to teaching and learning, to staying the course, and to holding their nerve while waiting for improvement. Beliefs match practice and practice matches beliefs throughout the system. It is daily practice for leaders and teachers to walk into classrooms and reflect on practice together. Newly hired teachers feel supported and woven into the learning culture through district-led coaching sessions and carefully selected mentors.

Coaching for performance improvement is a necessary part of realization. As Robertson (2005) has observed, leaders often feel they are in a reactive mode, responding within a context of ambiguity, paradox, and change and to a plethora of tasks characterized by brevity, complexity, and fragmentation. Leadership coaching is one approach to providing support to leaders by offering opportunities to have a dialogue, seek advice, rehearse, and question key instructional leadership decisions and actions. Leadership coaching provides a structure for thinking critically and reflectively, seeking support on leadership issues and practices, and becoming self-actualized, interdependent leaders.

Hiring practices throughout the district have well-defined criteria and precisely the same standards. Leaders who hire seek the most knowledgeable teaching staff and leaders with strong interpersonal skills whose strengths include a deep understanding of students as learners, assessment, and instruction, and whose passion and compassion are obvious. As a direct result, parents and students who must move to other areas are not penalized because classroom practice is consistent and variation has been diminished across all grades and courses.

INTERDEPENDENT PRACTICE AT THE SCHOOL LEVEL

Fear of changing direction and focus is never a worry because system and school improvement plans stay in place long after particular leaders leave, providing a stable and consistent focus. Conversely, the resolve for any leader, teacher, or support person to wait it out for the priority to pass is eliminated. Teachers and administrators pay attention to maximizing the number of minutes of instruction students receive. No student receives more in one school than another; they all receive the maximum

Honor walls are in classrooms where every student's best work is posted. Celebration walls are in hallways where Level 3 and 4 work by grade is posted. Performance walls are where student work is posted (or created by teacher/students), showing how to improve student achievement—last year we did this for the forms of writing.

(Laurie Welch, School Principal, Chatham, Ontario, personal communication, September 2008)

number of minutes of instructional time each day. Every classroom is a demonstration classroom where doors are open, teaching is public, and visitors and colleagues are expected to enter and learn together. Time is spent creating honor, celebration, and performance walls to make student learning visible.

Certainly these celebrations provide multiple signals of the developing personal platform for character education that cannot be taught, but that can be fostered by success and peer recognition. These celebrations contribute to creating high-energy school environments and interdependent practice. Here are some additional positive outcomes of interdependent practice:

- Students and teachers want to be at school, thus eliminating the dropout fear factor.
- All staff members are engaged in results-oriented action research as teams of teachers search for answers to assessment and instruction questions that arise when examining student work.
- Teachers bring students forward to time-tabled case management meetings to discuss how they can better meet and reach students' instructional needs. All take ownership of the students' progress and work on the cases until success is experienced by the teacher and students. Only then does the cycle repeat itself.
- Administrators and teachers invite parents and community members to be an integral part of the focus on students. Learning environments are redesigned by the use of new technologies that ensure continuous communication so that student learning at home and at school is seamless. Principals find ways to involve social agencies to support families and hire community liaison workers to focus on bringing parents and community members into the school to contribute to the learning environment. Parents and students see the school as a collection of resources for their own learning.

Teachers and leaders work on open communication with parents to bring about a change in attitude toward parents as important contributors to their children's education. One teacher put this succinctly: "We shifted away from what you often hear in schools as, well, you know, it's these children, their parents are never home, they never do anything with them."

> We will never get to full implementation (that is realization) until people really believe that all kids can learn. At our school no one would ever say anything about the students. We shifted from it's the fault of the kids to it's our problem, and ask ourselves what we need to do differently to make a change.
>
> (Kim Smith, System Principal, York Region District School Board, personal communication, August 2008)

INTERDEPENDENT PRACTICE AT THE CLASSROOM LEVEL

Strong, engaging interdependent practice holds the greatest promise for realization. Teachers move on from lesson study in guided practice to coteaching in interdependent practice as a very deep and intense strategy to further refine their knowledge of sound assessment and instructional practices.

> Full implementation (realization) reflects consistency in programs across grades and schools. That means research-based strategies are in place in all classrooms; data are used by classroom teachers, principals, and senior administration for planning and taking action; instruction is personalized to meet diverse student learning needs; students are engaged in lots of nonfiction writing across the curriculum; students are given tasks that reflect high expectations for all students; and students are achieving at or beyond standard in all curriculum expectations.
>
> (Ruth Mattingley, Senior Executive Officer, Ontario Literacy and Numeracy Secretariat, personal communication, August 2008)

Coteaching

In YRDSB, curriculum consultants who have formed trusting relationships with teachers in their intensive support schools find partner teachers to coteach with them. A coteaching partner could be a teacher in the same grade, the same division, the same school, or from central resource staff. During their time together, they do the following:

- Work side by side in real classroom environments
- Plan and discuss appropriate investigations based on assessment for learning data
- Analyze student work to guide instruction (data today is instruction tomorrow)
- Cofacilitate classroom discussions
- Examine and implement high-yield strategies based on data
- Reflect on their coteaching and joint work through the use of video and follow-up reflective discussion about what works, what doesn't work, and what they will do differently next time
- Examine video clips to look/listen for student work, student voice, questions, and critical thinking
- Plan next steps for student learning and teacher learning based on formative assessment, that is, working from where students are in their learning

The interdependent practice of coteaching helps teachers develop an understanding of how to use assessment data for differentiated instruction and the selection of the right resources for students. When the teaching force embraces this self-reflective teaching approach that we call coteaching, students, teachers, and administrators benefit immeasurably and we know that we have arrived at our destination: interdependence. Collaborative professional learning partnerships develop among coteachers in schools and among schools across districts. This brings cutting-edge, research-based supported instructional practice into classrooms.

To illustrate how deep and deliberate the reform has become, we consider a discussion with two curriculum consultants in YRDSB, Kathy Prince and Tracey Cox. They have found that the key to unlocking the going-deeper dilemma is using this powerful strategy of coteaching. This is a strong example of interdependent practice:

In our experience, coteaching is the most powerful way to improve our teaching practices and implement the changes in instruction that we've discussed, studied, and observed. In teaching, it's very difficult to assess our own progress, but in other disciplines such as horseback riding or dance we often work in environments where there are mirrors so that we can see the results of our efforts. In an arena outfitted with mirrors, we can see whether we have the horse bent correctly and "on the bit" and can observe whether our leg position is correct or needs altering.

In dance, we can see the arch of our back or the position of our hands. In both disciplines, minute changes are made constantly as a result of the analysis of our mirrored image. The challenge with teaching is that we have no mirrors. We cannot see ourselves and reflect upon our actions or our lesson in any objective way. We cannot replay the questions we ask or the prompts we give. We can't freeze a child's answer in order to think about what she really meant. Add to this the general "busy-ness" of schools: the number of activities, personalities, learning objectives, and incidents that crowd our day. The journey to become consciously skilled is daunting. The wonder is not that our progress is slow, but that we make any progress at all.

Coteaching is a way of providing us each with a mirror to our practice. When we coteach alongside a colleague, with the sole purpose of becoming a better teacher (increasingly skilled, reflective, and thoughtful), we provide the conditions necessary to be reflective, analytical, and thoughtful while learning with and from a respected colleague.

Our math team in YRDSB has delved deeply into what it means to teach and the teaching-learning cycle. As a result, we have formed explicit and focused coteaching relationships. On a personal note, Kathy Prince says that one of her most rewarding experiences has been coteaching with Shawn Perry, a young secondary mathematics teacher. Kathy had been a math consultant for two years, and Shawn had attended many of the workshop sessions she had conducted. He was always eager to ask questions, express an alternate view point, and read whatever was suggested. He had made significant shifts in his teaching, away from the traditional "stand and deliver" to teaching through problem solving, but he was not satisfied. In her role as a consultant, Kathy had learned a tremendous amount of theory, but did not have a place to try out new learning. At inservice sessions, she sometimes felt like an impostor advocating for teaching methods that she had not actually implemented in the classroom. Soon she found several teachers who graciously allowed her to come in and try new things. She would go in and teach the class, trying new problems, new minilessons, or new guiding questions. The teachers often left the class or simply sat back and watched. While this helped her develop her skills and be able to present to others with firsthand knowledge, it wasn't enough. She too felt dissatisfied with the arrangement.

As Shawn and Kathy developed a professional relationship, it quickly became apparent that they could learn from one another. They began their classroom work together by videotaping a three-part lesson over the course of three days. Then they watched the video together and set goals for themselves. Shawn was very interested in developing a math talk community and playing with the productive talk moves. Kathy was really interested in assessment for learning and using the math talk community to develop a better understanding of where students were in their mathematical understanding and how to move every student forward in his or her thinking.

Coteaching is changing our teachers' beliefs and understandings (parameter # 1). The cycle of collaboration and reflection has moved classroom practice from a focus on what is *taught* to a focus on what is *learned*.

(Kathy Prince, Curriculum Consultant, York Region District School Board, personal communication, December 2008)

Coteaching is a powerful way to learn together and to reflect on personal teaching practice. When we reflect upon our collective videotaped work, we can observe the impact of our actions on student learning. Together we set a goal aimed at improving our practice and make a plan to move student learning forward the very next day.

(Tracey Cox, Curriculum Consultant, York Region District School Board, personal communication, December 2008)

They have worked closely together ever since. Their coteaching has taken the form of reading the research together, planning lessons, teaching side by side, and videotaping lessons for analysis and discussion. They regularly engage in candid, open, and honest dialogue that questions their assumptions and reaches deeply into what it means to teach and learn. They are the mirror for each other, the mirror that helps them identify and understand the changes needed in their practice and in their beliefs. Together they have become increasingly skilled and wise.

As a result of going deeply into interdependent practice, Kathy and Shawn have embraced student voice during their coteaching. They meet with their students at the end of every semester and ask them to reflect on what worked or was challenging for them and what changes Kathy and Shawn could make to better meet their needs.

Realization is about the refinement of classroom teaching practice that is focused on student learning as illustrated in the preceding example of Kathy and Shawn. It is achieved when all teachers use precise and measurable goals to set high expectations and specific performance targets for each student, are clear about what they expect of every student, and are involved in their own goal setting as part of their learning process, in all classrooms. Then all students experience the alignment of the taught, learned, and assessed curriculum (Judy Speirs, Senior Student Achievement Officer, Ontario Literacy and Numeracy Secretariat, personal communication, August 2008), which provides them with predictability, confidence, and fairness. Student voice is heard more often than other voices in classrooms, creating resilient, outspoken learners who are prepared for life. There is visual evidence in all classrooms, at all levels, of strategies to help students make sense of what they read in all subject areas, for example word walls, posted exemplars, summary note section in student binders, posted explanations of EQAO terms, and seating that facilitates student discussion (Karen Timson, Mathematics Teacher, P. E. Trudeau SS, personal communication, August 2008).

Claxton (2002) summarizes the importance of having expectations that create interdependent practice:

> Realization occurs when students are happily engaged in their learning and are demonstrating growing independence and self-monitoring.
>
> (Judy Speirs, Senior Student Achievement Officer, Ontario Literacy and Numeracy Secretariat, personal communication, August 2008)

Students who are more confident of their own learning ability learn faster and learn better. They concentrate more, think harder, and find learning more enjoyable. Focusing on learning for everyone prepares youngsters better for an uncertain future. Today's schools are educating not just for exam results but for lifelong learning. To thrive in the twenty-first century, it is not enough to leave school with a clutch of examination certificates. You have to have learned how to be tenacious and resourceful, imaginative and logical, self-disciplined and self-aware, collaborative and inquisitive. (p. 1)

Full implementation looks like thoughtful, focused instructional practice grounded in the needs of students as indicated in the assessment data, what we know about how children learn and good teaching. It looks like a culture of learning where teams collaborate to find the best way to reach every student. Students focus on developing habits of mind necessary for success now and in future. There is a high level of engagement— parents, teachers, students, community are all focused on student achievement.

(Pauline Beder, Student Achievement Officer, Ontario Literacy and Numeracy Secretariat, personal communication, August 2008)

This quote reminds us of the ultimate goal for teachers and students: metacognition, or the ability to know how to learn and think. In realization, teachers raise the level of classroom discussion from just seeking one-word answers to engaging in higher-order dialogue (L. Sharratt, 1996). They offer students time to reflect and to voice their thinking, thus achieving metacognition. Michelle Prytula (2008) recently shared her doctoral dissertation on this very subject, stating that "through reflection, an individual has the opportunity to consider what he or she thinks and what others think. This thinking is then accelerated through dialogue, when the individual is called on to give voice to their thoughts. As the thinker experiences more opportunities to dialogue and reflect, he or she is provided with the opportunities to deconstruct and reconstruct what they believe and how they think . . . becoming aware of their own metacognition" (pp. 183–188).

In interdependent practice, through wait time, reflection, dialogue, and coteaching, metacognitive teaching results in students who are skilled self-assessors capable of

- Knowing and understanding what they are expected to learn
- Identifying their own strengths, needs, and interests
- Reflecting on their progress and setting goals
- Taking steps to improve their literacy learning
- Writing nonfiction with ease and coherence
- Advocating for themselves

Everyone's a Leader

We have not separated out leadership as a distinct category in this book. Instead, we have distributed the discussion of leadership throughout every scaffolded stage of our model. Having everyone take responsibility and be accountable for student learning outcomes enables sustainability of focus. Teachers and administrators, as cotransformational leaders in interdependent practice, use formative and summative assessment data to drive the precise selection of instructional strategies and resources (M. Sharratt, 2004). As a result of this integrated and purposeful interaction within and across districts, leaders become more aware of, and indeed more committed to, the success of all students in addition to their own. Figure 4.3 shows what we mean—leaders finding time to move from guided to interdependent practice.

Interdependent practice is recognized when virtually all administrators walk the talk and talk the walk.

Vignette: Bob Takes a Guided Reading Group (Parameters 1, 4, and 9 in Action)

Bob points out concepts of print, has Jimmy predict the storyline by looking at the pictures, and asks predicting and inferring questions of his small guided reading group (using leveled texts from their book room) to stretch their thinking. He challenges his small group of young, same-level readers to tackle the tough vocabulary before he begins reading with them and thinking together about the text. He uses their prior knowledge to build on new ideas that become new knowledge that they now understand and can use in talking with each other. Together they make text-to-text, text-to-self, and text-to-world connections with each other—almost forgetting that Bob is there. And who is Bob? He's the principal, and this is the best part of his daily literacy work in his school.

In the vignette, Bob is an example of instructional leadership in action and shows the seamlessness of interdependent leadership. He is part of his school team in which guided reading instruction is used as a sophisticated approach to differentiate instruction in the teaching of reading. Guided reading demands the ongoing assessment of students' reading levels beginning in Grade 1, and via differentiated instruction this approach continues throughout elementary school. Students with similar reading levels are brought together in small flexible groupings, moving on as their reading level increases. Students who are struggling receive daily reading practice in these guided reading groups. Figures 4.4 and 4.5 are samples of laminated guided reading file folders that teachers and administrators

Figure 4.3   Leadership Capacity Building That Leads to Leadership Realization

Leadership Capacity Building (out-of-school professional learning)	Leadership Realization (in-school working interdependently)
Leaders at every level engage in district literacy walk and coaching conversation training that occurs in schools to learn with colleagues.	Administrators conduct literacy walks daily in their schools and periodically engage in coaching conversations by asking reflective questions of each other and teachers. Teachers walk in and out of each other's classrooms as critical friends/coaches.
Action research (AR) inquiry skills are acquired by leaders being trained at all levels.	School staff members engage in collaborative inquiry based on a variety of school data. AR annual report (and presentation of it) shows evidence of student improvement in answering the focused AR question.
District literacy leadership team professional learning sessions and learning networks/communities focus on change management theory, 13 parameters, and demonstration of them in successful classroom practices.	Learning from PL sessions extends to and impacts practice of all classroom teachers and makes a difference in the instruction for all students.
The district sets up demonstration classrooms so that teachers and administrators visit together, observe, discuss, and plan for action.	Administrators and teachers visit demonstration classrooms multiple times during the year to reflect on instructional decisions that are being made based on emerging data; then they discuss and apply what they learn to practice in every classroom in their own school.

use as prompts and anecdotal observation tools when working with students. These folders are very useful in making the critical move from a low-level round-robin reading approach to the higher instructional approach of guided reading. Note the emphasis on solid literacy instructional practices such as making connections and using higher-order questioning in the sample folders. Teachers and administrators use anecdotal notes on observation sheets, stored in the folders, to record ongoing improvement of all students' reading fluency and comprehension and make note of what other practice is needed.

In concluding this chapter, we like Pfeffer and Sutton's (2006) observation about Toyota, that over their decades of success Toyota "shows *no leadership effects*" (p. 211, italics in the original). By this they mean that interdependent practice is so embedded and reinforced by so many interlocking people and actions that given leaders could come and go without there being any negative impact. Toyota's culture had a built-in capacity to replenish itself. This is realization.

Here's the problem, in too many schools we think implementation means a few enthusiastic people doing it. . . . Don't say that we're doing collaboration, for example, if we don't have 90% of our faculty consistently, collaboratively scoring student work. Don't say that we're using high-yield teaching strategies, such as questions or cues or advanced organizers or similes and metaphors, if 90% of our faculty doesn't use them on a regular basis.

(D. Reeves, Teacher Moderation: Collaborative Assessment of Student Work, September 10, 2007, Ontario Literacy and Numeracy Secretariat Webcast).

Figure 4.4   Sample Guided Reading Folder (Outside)

SYNTHESIZING TEXT

- What did you learn about this topic?
- Was there anything that you thought you knew about the topic, but after reading this text has changed your mind?
- What do you already know about this topic?

GUIDED READING PROMPTS

- Use sticky notes when reading so you don't lose your thought.
- Reread constantly to find new information.
- Write down difficult vocabulary so you can look it up later.
- Write down any question you have so you don't forget them during a guided reading lesson.
- Describe the setting of the text.
- How did the author begin the text to engage the reader?
- What is the theme?
- Read aloud significant quotes.
- Make predictions about what happens next.
- Did anything puzzle you?
- Identify the genre of the book and what makes it that genre.
- Make any connections: text to text, text to self and text to world.
- Identify any character that you are drawn to or with whom you feel a connection.
- Identify any connections to T.V. or movies.
- What you are learning from this book?
- Who is the most important/interesting character?
- How does the character change in the book?
- What was the mood or atmosphere?
- How do the characters feel about one another?
- What is the problem in the text? How did you think it would be resolved?
- What lessons does this text teach about life?

FIX-UP STRATEGIES

- What problem-solving strategies did you use?
- Were you reading effectively? How do you know?
- What did you learn . . . ?
- What did you think about . . . ?
- Why did you decide . . . ?
- What tells you that . . . ?
- Does this make sense . . . ?
- Did you know something about this topic before reading the book?
- Does it fit in with what you already know about . . . ?

Source: Copyright © M. Sharratt, York Region District School Board, 2005.

VISUALIZING

- Describe the main character in your story. You can use illustrations to support your answer.
- Where and when does the story take place? Describe what you see in your mind when you read the book. Use evidence from the book to support your answer.
- What would a map of the area look like?

DETERMINING IMPORTANT IDEAS

- What is the author's message in this story? Why do you think he\she wrote the story?
- Talk about an important decision that a character in your book had to make. Do you agree or disagree with their decision as the solution to their problem?
- What are the most important ideas presented in the story?

QUESTIONING

- What are some questions you have for the author?
- Were there parts of the book you didn't understand? What puzzles you?
- Did you have any questions about the book that were answered as you continued to read?
- List at least 3 questions that you have and try to guess/predict the answers.

MAKING CONNECTIONS

- Does this book make you think about an event that happened in your life, a relationship that you have, or a decision that you had to make?
- Does this story remind you of anything that is going on in our world today?
- Does this story remind you of a movie, a television program, or another book that you have read?

MAKING INFERENCES

- Make a guess on how a character in the story is feeling after an important event in the story. What in the book makes you think this?
- How did the characters feel about one another?
- What do you think will happen next in the story?
- How do you think the story's problem or conflict will be fixed?
- What do you think a character in the book is going to do next in the story?
- Did you hope an event in the story wouldn't happen, but it happened anyway?
- Was it easy to predict the events of the plot? Were there any clues about what was going to happen next?

Figure 4.5 Sample Guided Reading Folder (Inside)

CONNECTION

TEXT TO TEXT

- Does this remind you of another book?
- How is this book alike/different from another book by the same author?
- Is the vocabulary in the book similar to that in another book?
- Have you read a book about a setting like this before?
- Do you know of another book with the same theme? Which one?
- Do the illustrations remind you of another book?
- Can you think of another book in the same genre?

TEXT TO SELF

- How would you to solve this problem?
- What image comes to mind when you think about...?
- What would you do in the same situation?
- Has something like this ever happened to you?
- Have you ever experienced this?
- How did it make you feel?
- Have you ever felt this way?
- Would you ever do this?
- Do you agree with what the character did? Why?

TEXT TO WORLD

- Does this remind you of something that happened in the news?
- Is this the same as... (an event or real life situation)?
- Has this ever happened before? When? Where?

A COLLECTION OF PROMPTS FOR RESPONDING TO TEXTS

NARRATIVE TEXTS

1. What is the author's message?
2. What is the story really about?
3. Do you think the title is appropriate for the story?
4. Why do you think the author wrote this story?
5. Are different points of view presented?
6. What are some of the most important ideas?
7. Were there parts of the book you didn't understand? What puzzled you?
8. What question(s) do you still have?
9. What does this text want you to learn more about?
10. Who was the voice the author chose as narrator – first person, third person, storyteller, an anonymous voice, a different voice, or the author him- or herself?
11. Did this style work well?
12. What was the more important, the plot or the characters?
13. Are the family relationships presented in a stereotypical way?
14. Where and when does the story take place?
15. Where else could the story take place?
16. Could the setting be a real place that exists in our time?
17. How much time passes in this story?
18. In another time or place, how would the story change?
19. How did the author control the passing of time?
20. Does the setting change over the person's life?
21. What was the mood or atmosphere of the story, or did it change as you read the book?
22. Are there any powerful characters in the story? What makes them that way?
23. Who is the most important character?
24. Who is the most interesting character?
25. Which character taught you the most?
26. How does the author/illustrator reveal the character? (Look at what the character does, thinks, or says, and what others say about the character.)
27. Which characters change and which didn't? How is character change important in the story?
28. Who is the character that plays a small role? Why is this character necessary in the story?
29. What did you learn from one character in the story?
30. How did the characters feel about one another?
31. What changes do the characters encounter and how do they deal with them?
32. What choices did the characters have?

CHAPTER FIVE

The Devil Is in the Details

Beware of the Pitfalls!

In Chapter 2 we wrote about the 13 parameters that form the basis of consistent and powerful capacity building. Through these conditions, we discussed a gradual release-of-responsibility model of learning (modeled, shared, guided, interdependent) that brings learning organizations to realization. With the 13 parameters and the model of four learning progressions in place as screens, let's sift through some of what we have heard, observed, and read from contributors in preparing this text. And we have heard it all!

"I'm not in control and I'm the leader!"

This book is about just that: the gradual release of responsibility from modeling to sharing to guiding and finally to interdependent practice. This learning progression takes vision and reflection to see beyond the present reality and know when to allow systems, districts, schools, and/or teachers to fly confidently on their own and to trust their new skills. We say to those internal or external leaders who hold on to power and who thereby pass their "best before" date, it is challenging and necessary work to step back and let the learners step up—and excel, often beyond what we thought was possible. And by the way, you will also learn, and you will extend your "best before" date. This is truly realization. Those who can't let go with confidence become obstacles for the system, the school, or the classroom teacher in becoming interdependent. Everyone is susceptible to hanging onto control and must self-evaluate how to let go and how to celebrate the release of responsibility earned.

"What about obesity?"

Not understanding where content fits within curriculum expectations can take governments, districts, and schools off track. It's very easy to get sidetracked with the latest new thing or media event, and there are many special interest groups in the teaching population who can and will create an alphabet soup of causes that will sidetrack you from the real alphabet and numbers. Let us say it again: understanding and staying the course is tough work that demands knowledge and strength of commitment and the ability to manage distracters.

Obesity content, for example, is part of our health and well-being curriculum expectation. But teaching the content and its implications and ensuring that assessment and instruction through the lens of literacy is considered—is a level above the content—is our overall strategy. To take our eye off the "assessment that drives instruction" ball and switch to something else, such as obesity, complete with distracting funding, is a deterrent to our students' success. You can't do it all. Being able to narrow the focus of the priority, stay the course, and articulate why we are not "doing obesity" is doable.

"We don't know why our scores have plummeted. We're working so hard."

Not knowing why and not doing anything to find out why are gateways to giving up on kids and teachers. There are many ways to get whatever support is required to analyze the data in order to determine what the students are and are not being taught. Working smarter, not harder, applies here. Being precise, focused, and specific about classroom practice is key. Having too much going on in a school or district and trying to do it all are enemies to system, school, and student improvement. Getting started in peeling back the data and letting the data decide sometimes requires outside assistance. Knowing where to seek help is part of that will, perseverance, and resiliency we talk about. In the same vein, not knowing what to do with failing kids is tragic. We need to put aside the pretty plans and "surfacey" discussions in order to scrutinize individual student work—in a case management approach—to find instructional solutions together (Parameter 6, see Chapter 2).

"I wonder why parents want this
Grade 5 class but not the others."

We have written and spoken often about variance among classroom practices. Parents and other teachers know the differences between successful and poor classroom practice. Parents petition or make their choices for success over mediocrity in many different ways, often subtly, such as opting for French immersion or specialized arts or sports programs. Often their reaction is not so subtle. You know the signs, but do you know how to interpret and deal with them? Teachers with high expectations and joyous learning environments, where student voices are heard most often, are in high demand by astute parents. Hiring carefully and then giving time and the right support to all teachers will lessen principals' need to deal with declining enrollment or angry parent delegations. Tightening capacity building and realization puts effective support and pressure on all teachers to improve.

"We have no time."

Every educational book ever written cites time as a deterrent to increasing student achievement. It amazes us how the theme survives in some provinces/states, districts, and schools while not in others. Why can some find the time to get focused on the important things that make a difference and others can't? Some activities promulgated as new collaborative tools may waste time if theory is misinterpreted. We have said that learning networks can make a difference—but not learning networks that take one year to decide on a focus, aren't focused on reaching all 8,800 teachers, or can't agree on the collaborative leadership style needed to move forward. The urgency is made crystal clear when we think about the teachers and kids who are not being reached while we waste precious time taking baby steps or deciding who will lead. Often it is better to "ready, fire, aim." Just doing it and making midcourse corrections is often the best way forward. Learning networks may offer distributed leadership opportunities; however, they are not organizations unto their own.

Putting aside ego in leadership takes time as well. We have often talked about minimizing hierarchical formal leadership to embrace knowledgeable leadership in order to learn together. Principals need to walk alongside or just behind literacy coaches in some cases where knowledge is needed, and that's not a bad thing. But it takes strength to overcome feelings of inadequacy, to put aside ego in order to learn. If there isn't a lot of time, where do we focus our energy? Observing others, whether during literacy walks, demonstration classrooms visits, lesson study, or coteaching, is a powerful strategy in moving forward together, but observing and learning from others definitely takes humility to do authentically. Recognizing that there is more to learn is often the first step in leadership self-assessment. Then spending time learning with the best practitioners is a fruitful use of leaders' time.

"This is how we work. The new way doesn't work. We couldn't possibly change! We've tried it."

Bumping up against culture is commonly heard in relation to structures that get in the way, such as time tables, the way schools are built, staffing allocations, unions demanding no professional learning at staff meetings, or balkanized departments in secondary schools. It takes real knowledge of how students learn to understand what, how, and why some structures get in the way of improvement. Then it takes a commitment of energy to remove them. Often the first leadership steps that should be taken are those that are against the current of popular culture at staff meetings, board tables, district visioning sessions, and in staff rooms. On those occasions, it's often easier and jazzier for leaders to be seen as collaborative than for them to take the more difficult stance of staying the course.

Politics at every level can interfere with the development of positive cultures needed to focus on our core business: increasing student achievement. Ill-conceived accountability provisions by central policy makers create diversions as they place emphasis on the wrong things. Negative directions from unions trying to maintain the status quo are detrimental to the collegiality and harmony that need to be created and experienced by all. Relationship building is a key (as evidenced in the Chapter 3 story about including union leaders in literacy walk training). However, leadership mandates are often necessary and helpful for all to move forward. As we have seen, a clear message of what we believe in and why we are doing what we are doing—in the district and at all our schools—is often in order. And mandates work. Stating a mandate requires clear and informed thinking, courage of conviction, and courageous conversations (as discussed in the Chapter 3 section on Reading Recovery). Executing the mandated priority requires focused leadership energy to weather the storms of special interests, unions, or the powerful inertia of previously goal-less staff.

Knowing the potential of the people you are working with in your buildings is strategic leadership. Growing your own leaders and teachers and encouraging their continuously improving classroom professionalism are important leadership strategies. This is exemplified in the following case study that highlights overcoming the many challenging circumstances mentioned in this section.

CROSBY HEIGHTS PUBLIC SCHOOL CASE STUDY

Crosby Heights is a K–8 school of 662 students in a low-income neighborhood in a growing York Region community. It was designated by the district as a Performance Plus School over the years, that is, a school in challenging circumstances requiring attention. After five years of focused work, the principal, Ryan Friedman, and his team have overcome the following obstacles to begin producing the impressive results shown in Figure 5.1:

- No focal point (lack of clear vision)*
- Toxic culture (negative culture)
- A facility that was in poor shape, with nonfunctional lighting, paint peeling, nonexistent or torn blinds, a shabby play yard, and drafty windows (structural barriers)
- Demoralized unionized staff (negative culture)
- Unsafe school environment, including violence and oppositional students (negative culture)
- Critical parents wanting to get their children out (negative culture)
- Huge discrepancy between report card results and provincial standardized assessments, indicating that assessments did not match curriculum expectations (assessment and instruction issues)
- Lack of common language regarding instruction (assessment and instruction issues)
- Low achievement on the provincial assessment (assessment and instruction issues)

---

*The categorization in parentheses is our way of organizing Ryan's actions using the five factors or conditions that principals must consider when developing schools as a learning organization (Leithwood, Leonard, & Sharratt, 2000).

The ongoing commitment and engagement of the Board's senior staff with the union has proven to have been invaluable in promoting and sustaining positive labour relations and a focus on student achievement. This commitment to engaging and collaborating with secondary union officials includes

- routine informal contact (telephone, e-mail) several times weekly;
- formal meetings held two to three times monthly on topics related to personnel matters, program, staffing, policy and procedure, and school operations; and
- union leader membership on key Board committees (Assessment and Evaluation, Student Success, Digital Literacy, Board Planning, etc.).

The Board and union commitment to inclusive leadership has enabled the most significant of differences to be resolved proactively, constructively, and amicably; grievances are rare and filed on impasse and as a last resort. Our focus on student achievement is enhanced and sustained through this approach.

(Bob Harper, Coordinating Superintendent of Education, York Region District School Board, personal communication, April 2009)

In the years before there was a forward plan (2000–2001 to 2004–2005), student performance as measured by the provincial assessment agency was low and jumping around in a nonlinear manner. Ryan entered as principal in 2004. In the following three years, the school dramatically increased the percentage of its students in Grades 3 and 6 achieving the province's demanding proficiency level (3 or 4 on a 4-point scale).

Figure 5.1 shows the results in Grade 6 reading, writing, and math compared with the scores of the *same* students when they were in Grade 3. Note the significant and impressive 33 percent to 47 percent increase in the Grade 3 students achieving Level 3 and 4 from 2004–2005 to 2007–2008.

How did this happen? Crosby Heights is one example of how a principal and his team, with district support, implemented the 13 parameters. As a new principal in 2004, Ryan quickly established a

Figure 5.1   Increase in Crosby Heights Students Achieving Level 3 or 4, 2004–2007*

	Baseline Year: 2004–2005 As Grade 3 Students	Year 3: 2007–2008 As Grade 6 Students	Baseline to Year 3: % Increase by Same Students
Reading	44%	90%	46%
Writing	40%	87%	47%
Mathematics	50%	83%	33%

*EQAO (See also Figure 4.1.)

vision for his school that mirrored the district's vision and priority of literacy. He shared this vision and priority every chance he got and made time to meet all his teachers, working with them at whatever level they were at in their professional lives. His personal version of the district vision for the school amounted to five nuggets:

- Learning for all, whatever it takes
- All equals *all*
- Students and staff can articulate their potential
- A focus on literacy, that is, balanced literacy
- Excellence in all that we do

He clearly articulated the vision to staff and found ways to share it everywhere, including newsletters to staff and parents, presentations at parents' nights and school council meetings, and focused learning for staff on professional activity days. Over time, after the teachers had begun to experience success in the classroom, Ryan felt safe sharing the following beliefs and understandings more explicitly, looking for buy-in:

- All students can achieve at high levels given adequate time, the right support, and effective instruction and resources
- High achievement is not an accident
- We are all responsible for all of the students
- Equity does not mean equality
- Be responsible for your own actions
- Share decision making
- Practice an ethic of care and mutual respect

- Provide an emotionally and physically safe and supportive learning environment

Ryan then set about to model, share, and guide practice so his staff would become interdependent, that is, achieve realization. He became even more precise about the literacy focus and guided his staff, through pressure and support, toward four key goals:

- Creating proficient, independent readers and writers
- Understanding that reading and writing are the important parts of the curriculum
- Understanding that reading and writing work across all subject areas
- Having students see themselves as readers, authors, critics, researchers, and artists

Ryan knew that his own attitude and performance were his most powerful tools, so he modeled those beliefs consistently for staff. Because of that positive influence, and the resulting willingness to work with him, teachers came to share the beliefs slowly but steadily, and eventually Ryan broke the previously toxic school environment.

> When dealing with union issues, I try to listen attentively, behave with integrity, act with conviction, and keep moving forward with perseverance.
>
> (Ryan Friedman, Principal, Crosby Heights Public School, personal communication, April 2009)

To their professional credit, the school staff members who stayed the course have become inspirational to each other and to other school teams. Subtly and not so subtly, Ryan believes that he changed beliefs and understandings in a number of ways:

- Establishing job-embedded learning, that is, right in the school, with staff as a professional learning community between the bells; he stayed true to his course, saying, "Professional learning is not an option here at Crosby Heights" (culture)*

---

* Similar to our earlier note, the categorization in parentheses represents five key conditions to consider when evaluating schools as effective learning organizations (Leithwood et al., 2000, pp. 99–124).

- Building relationships with teachers and support staff and the school community (culture)
- Transferring a few teachers who struggled to buy into the vision (vision and structure)
- Modeling hope, optimism, life-long learning, and caring for others (culture)
- Having high expectations of teachers to rise to the teaching challenge (assessment and instruction)
- Providing needed resources for teachers (resources)
- Celebrating small incremental successes (vision and assessment and instruction)
- Seizing opportunities daily, weekly, and monthly through constant newsletters to teachers and parents to remind staff, parents, community to stay the course (structure)
- Staying current with research on the most successful practices to increase school and student improvement—and then applying the research he found (assessment and instruction)
- Doing whatever it takes to get additional resources, whether it was speaking to the superintendent of schools, the plant department, or the Reading Recovery teacher-leader (resources)
- Putting in place multiple teams to distribute the leadership and to accept the responsibility for teachers' practice and student improvement (structure)
- Changing the attitudes of teachers, students, staff, parents, and district leaders to understand that improvement could happen at Crosby Heights (culture)

One can see that Ryan and his leadership team found ways to embrace our pressure-and-support mantra—to guide the learning—in turning around this large school. He is an unabashed, informed risk taker who routinely asks for staff feedback on his leadership. One young staff member commented:

[The principal] does an excellent job of promoting and reinforcing a shared sense of purpose. He uses data to inform us of the progress toward our goal, sends articles to read to enhance our PD [professional development], and lets us know about district workshops that we may want to attend. He is very approachable and easy to talk to about issues, concerns, or questions that I have as a first-year teacher. His caring about the needs of his staff is greatly appreciated and admired. He trusts us as educators in our field and in our ability to make good decisions. When he feels strongly about an issue, he is very diplomatic in his delivery of his point of view, which contributes to his respect of others and his approachable nature.

Another teacher on staff who has been at the school for a long time commented positively as well:

[He] is consistently approachable and visible within the school. He works hard to resolve conflicts and build good relationships with staff and students. He is respectful of others as demonstrated in his mannerisms, language, and actions. He encourages teachers to take on new leadership roles, involves community and family participation in the school, and most definitely demonstrates a deep knowledge of teaching and the learning process. I admire the fact that he is constantly willing to learn new things and share what he has learned with others. His use of data to drive instruction has helped us all see that this is an important tool. He has built consensus around the school plan and delivers on his commitments. He has made a significant change in our school and made it such a positive place to be.

Ryan himself says that all the improvements and positive comments are due to the contribution of his staff members. He notes that school improvement starts in the classroom surrounded by the 13 parameters (see Chapter 2) working in concert. However, our research says that two arenas must come together in improvement at every level: first a focus on classroom practice, followed by leadership with pressure and support. Ryan has had no end of questioning about how he accomplished the improvements to date and continues to maintain energy for his school and students. One of his staff members, who is working on her master's degree, wrote a paper about his leadership style, in which she answered the questions:

I chose to interview Mr. Friedman, because in my opinion, he is such an awe-inspiring, dynamic, and results-oriented principal. Since he joined our school three years ago, he has brought about many changes that not only have worked (affectively) [sic], but have also improved student learning scores (empirically). He was able to bring about those changes by motivating the staff, getting them on board with the ideas, and then charting the path for them. All along the way, he would continue to support the staff, listen to them, and empower them. (Datoo, 2006, p. 1)

Through the gradual-release-of-responsibility learning model (modeled, shared, guided, and interdependent practice), Ryan led the staff to experience school and student improvement. There wasn't just one single silver bullet or one single action that he took to overcome all the obstacles he initially faced. It was a concerted leadership effort to delve deeply into each of the 13 parameters (see Chapter 2) that has resulted in interdependent practice at Crosby Heights.

Ryan may be one of the better school leaders in York Region, but this is a matter of degree, not kind. Our capacity-building-to-realization model has systematically engaged all leaders, teachers, and students. Aligned leadership at the district and school levels is a key to staying and deepening the course, and this too is consistent. Not coincidentally, such alignment and deep implementation results in a very powerful wave of a thousand and more change agents who have tasted success and "want more, please." They will not be satisfied with less.

Vignette: Literacy Is the "Language of the Discipline" at Every Grade and in Every Course of Study—Not Just in Primary School (Parameters 1 and 13 in Action)

Grade 12 science teacher Sarah is a master teacher. How do we know? She believes that every teacher is a literacy teacher; she tells her colleagues that scientific literacy is important for students to understand the terms and know how science will affect their lives. She makes the learning expectations for her students explicit—up front—at the beginning of every lesson. Sarah gives her students a rationale for her lesson, tied to the curriculum expectations as well as to a real-life application that they will experience outside of school, saying things like "Before you leave here, my goal is to get you ready to read scientific journal articles, be able to make notes, know how to code for importance, organize your thoughts, and understand the stuff."

Using graphic organizers, focused questions to hear her students' voices, and effective data-based groupings for project-based classroom work, Sarah enthusiastically challenges students to *begin* as readers and writers and to *become* critical thinkers and problem solvers. She competently covers the curriculum in meaningful and energizing ways by using graphic organizers, experimenting with academic controversy as one example of many higher-order instructional strategies, and integrating the use of technologies as powerful instructional and motivational tools. Her formative assessment practices allow students to continually strive for excellence by giving students many second chances to improve, building assessment rubrics together so that they understand what her expectations are, and giving students time to improve daily before giving final summative grades. Word walls display the language of the unit being taught as one visual cue, daily and weekly reminders are visible, and lesson agendas allow everyone to see how the lesson will unfold. Not a minute of instructional time is wasted.

And what do her students say? "I definitely will use her strategies, like graphic organizers, in other classes that I have. Her way of teaching helps me organize my thoughts and be able to think more deeply about the concepts."

THE PARAMETERS SCAFFOLDED

Figure 5.2 summarizes the parameters in action across the four phases of scaffolded learning—modeled, shared, guided, and interdependent practice. (For the sake of completion, we have had to get a bit ahead of ourselves by including the 14th parameter, which we turn to in Chapter 6.)

We advise school and district leaders to first attend to the four big-picture ideas (see Chapter 1): What should be the area of focus (we recommend literacy deeply defined)? What is the current state of performance according to student achievement data? How can leadership be initially aligned (school, district, state)? How can parents and the community be connected, at least by discussing the direction of the reforms with them?

Second, we recommend that school and district leaders seek to understand the gist of the parameters and especially their interaction, that is, how they operate in concert.

The third task is to commit to the journey of going deeper and deeper into practice—in effect, scaffolding learning through more systematic, planned, and consistent practice. This gets back to Malcolm Gladwell's (2008) idea of ten thousand hours (or our revised thirty thousand hours). There is no substitute for hard, purposeful work. The pursuit of instructional improvement involves a combination of relentless consistency (of proven practices) and continuous improvement (through innovation and new ideas from within the system, and externally in the broader field of research and practice).

Now we can turn to the 14th parameter—shared responsibility and accountability—the social glue of realization.

Figure 5.2 Matrix of Scaffolded Learning

PARAMETER	MODELED PRACTICE	SHARED PRACTICE	GUIDED PRACTICE	INTERDEPENDENT PRACTICE
1. Shared Beliefs and Understandings	▪ District and school leaders and teachers articulate vision everywhere, at any time (professional development sessions, staff meetings, board meetings).	▪ Leaders and teachers work in smaller clusters or networks with "accountable talk," i.e., teachers can articulate why and how they teach what they do.	▪ All teachers receive intensive and ongoing training focused on classroom practice (e.g., literacy walks, Reading Recovery, Action Research, and lesson study).	▪ Special education and regular education assessment and instruction are seamless; all students are engaged and achieving, and all parents are involved.
▪ All students can achieve high standards given sufficient time and the right support.	▪ They use data in the district and schools to set targets; intervention practices are in place in all schools.	▪ They discuss how to use data to differentiate instruction; intervention techniques are discussed and in place at every level.	▪ Teachers moderate student work; performance targets are visible in every classroom.	▪ The case management approach is used for each struggling student; all students can articulate performance targets and their work to be done.
▪ High expectations and early and ongoing intervention are essential.	▪ Administrators and literacy leads model and work alongside classroom teachers.	▪ They use video clips to discuss best practices and build on clips.	▪ Literacy coaches now demonstrate embedded assessment and instructional strategies and model descriptive feedback.	▪ Teachers (and administrators) coteach, question as critical friends, and examine students' thinking.
▪ All teachers can teach to high standards given the right assistance.	▪ Teachers can articulate to colleagues and parents why they are instructing as they are.	▪ Teachers share practice through demonstration class visits, opening their doors.	▪ Teachers plan and watch each other teach (lesson study) and demonstrate student improvement using samples of student work.	▪ Students can articulate why and how they learn, using the same language and evidence from their work.
▪ Teachers can articulate what they do and why they teach the way they do.				

PARAMETER	MODELED PRACTICE	SHARED PRACTICE	GUIDED PRACTICE	INTERDEPENDENT PRACTICE
2. **Embedded Literacy Coaches**	■ Partial staffing is allocated during school day to model successful literacy instruction in every school. ■ Selection is critical: they must be "knowledgeable others," credible, supportive, approachable.	■ Ongoing dialogue with principal and leadership team focuses on school and student data.	■ Districts find the funding to hire/carefully select literacy coaches in every school ■ Literacy coaches work alongside classroom teachers in planning. They demonstrate literacy assessment and instructional practices during the literacy block. ■ They demonstrate how technology is an integral instructional tool.	■ Step back—lead from behind. ■ Students consistently use strategies and skills; teachers and literacy coaches support when necessary. ■ Literacy coaches coteach with teachers across all divisions to refine practice and focus on students' thinking.
3. **Time-Tabled Literacy Block**	■ Minimum 100-minute block is time-tabled for literacy instruction. ■ Minimum 60-minute block is time-tabled for mathematics instruction. ■ Interruptions are eliminated during literacy block and time is protected for instruction.	■ Literacy instruction progresses from modeled to shared to guided to interdependent. ■ Teachers move from whole-to small-group to individual differentiated literacy instruction.	■ Data determine which students need more daily guided practice. ■ Assessment informs all instruction. ■ Literacy skills are observed and demonstrated through lesson study sessions. ■ Higher-order questions promote critical thinking.	■ Students' voice is heard frequently. ■ Students work independently using explicit, timely formative feedback from teachers' assessments (e.g., one praise point and one instructional point). ■ Students use multiple forms of technology to demonstrate their literacy learning.

(Continued)

Figure 5.2 (Continued)

PARAMETER	MODELED PRACTICE	SHARED PRACTICE	GUIDED PRACTICE	INTERDEPENDENT PRACTICE
4. **Principal Leadership**	■ Principals can articulate deep, structured understanding of assessment that drives literacy instruction for all staff. ■ They use technology for effectiveness and efficiency. ■ They have an instructional coach if needed.	■ Principals are part of literacy leadership team and attend PL with staff; no other priority is more important to spend time on. ■ Superintendents, curriculum staff, and principals lead PL sessions.	■ Principals and staff use data to drive school plans and guide selection of resources and instructional strategies. ■ They provide focused PL and resources that reflect district sessions.	■ Principals and teachers support all students' learning through frequent, nonevaluative classroom literacy walks and follow-up reflective conversations about practice. ■ They ensure that all teachers and students have opportunities to learn with and through appropriate technology.
5. **Early and Ongoing Intervention**	■ Data are used to identify struggling students' strengths and areas of need early in each school year at every grade level in order to put interventions in place immediately.	■ Assessment data are shared with all teachers in order to make collaborative decisions about how to move all struggling learners forward.	■ Guided instructional training, in literacy interventions such as Reading Recovery, is provided for some teachers who form first cohort, and a systematic plan is developed to provide training for all teachers in district over a five-year period.	■ Wait lists are a thing of the past—no students wait! All students are actively engaged in relevant and appropriate learning. ■ Students use technology to support their individual differentiated learning.

PARAMETER	MODELED PRACTICE	SHARED PRACTICE	GUIDED PRACTICE	INTERDEPENDENT PRACTICE
6. **Case Management Approach**	■ Administrators and literacy leadership teams gather, triangulate, and report data for schools and students. ■ Display performance data (tracking walls, data folders, smart boards, etc.) for staff to discuss and take collective responsibility for all students' improvement.	■ Teachers identify which students they need instructional help with. ■ Time tables reflect that specialist teachers in school provide instruction in classrooms to free up classroom teachers to attend case management meetings.	■ Principals, literacy coaches, and classroom teachers come together in scheduled case management meetings during the school day. ■ Classroom teachers present struggling students' work for collective problem solving. ■ The team recommends instructional strategies to try, taking ownership.	■ Teachers implement instructional strategies recommended in case management meetings. ■ They return to follow-up meetings until student improvement is achieved. ■ Many or all students benefit from the strategies tried for one student.
7. **Literacy Professional Development at School Staff Meetings**	■ Principals and literacy leadership teams as lead-learners model district key messages and embed PL from district sessions at all staff meetings.	■ Principals, literacy leads, and teachers, using diagnostic data, determine staff learning needs and lead differentiated PL. ■ Teachers use technology to get just-in-time personal literacy PL beyond the PL at staff meetings.	■ Principals and literacy coaches use school data to identify the parameter(s) that need focused PL (Parameter 1 is most challenging and is always a given). ■ They develop a key AR question that reflects the parameters chosen (see Parameter 11) and work on finding answers all year.	■ Beliefs match practice and become a habit of mind. ■ School and classroom learning environments are characterized by high energy, staff room conversations focus on students' improvement, and students use common language modeled by K–12 teachers.

Figure 5.2 (Continued)

PARAMETER	MODELED PRACTICE	SHARED PRACTICE	GUIDED PRACTICE	INTERDEPENDENT PRACTICE
8. In-School Grade/Subject Meetings	■ Literacy leads/department heads model what literacy looks like in all curriculum areas at every large- and small-group teacher and administrative meeting; operational issues are reduced to memo format.	■ Weekly discussions of student work at grade or division meetings lead to common language and understanding of curriculum expectation and explicit assessment that informs instructional strategies. ■ Teachers have common planning time to collaboratively assess student work and reach consensus through rich dialogue on the level of each piece of work.	■ Administrators and literacy coaches build and share a varied repertoire of high-yield assessment and instructional strategies to support teachers. ■ Teachers learn from each other by modeling what is working for them; they visit other classrooms together to see others' practice and discuss refining their own.	■ Students benefit from immediate, explicit feedback from teachers about their work and are given on-the-spot instruction to move them forward.
9. Book Rooms With Leveled Books and Resources	■ Administrators, literacy leads, and teacher-librarians collect school resources and locate them in a central location for all teachers to use. ■ Analyze gaps to determine what further resources are needed.	■ Teachers share the use of leveled texts and multidimensional resources, all appropriately labeled according to the stage learners are at. ■ Resources are also categorized by authors, genres, and publishers, and include graphic novels, bibliographies, software, etc. ■ Administrators and teachers select professional resource books to read and discuss at book study	■ Literacy coaches and teachers collaboratively plan and teach lessons using a variety of resources and instructional approaches. ■ Teachers use software to discuss, share, and guide use of exemplary resources with others.	■ Students see themselves reflected in the classroom resources used. ■ Students know how to use web technology to find resources and information and know how to apply use. ■ Students share their resources in collaboratively designed group work with built-in individual student accountability.

PARAMETER	MODELED PRACTICE	SHARED PRACTICE	GUIDED PRACTICE	INTERDEPENDENT PRACTICE
10. **Allocation of District and School Budgets for Literacy Learning and Resources**	■ Senior management and elected officials (trustees) continue to fund literacy resources (human and material) in tough economic times by finding operational areas to cut costs; they are united in staying the course.	■ District curriculum consultants share how to use resources and instructional approaches, using blended learning model (face-to-face time and interactive technology time) to reach all teachers. ■ Teachers in small groups are expected to try out resources and apply their new skills to refine their practice.	■ Literacy coaches support the selection and use of resources for classrooms and book rooms. ■ Carefully selected resources mirror the diversity in classrooms and enable students to see themselves in them.	■ Equity of outcomes for all students is experienced and acknowledged through data—all students are meeting the high performance targets set for them. ■ Students, parents, and the community see schools as resources for their own learning; schools find many contextually unique ways to accomplish this.
11. **Action Research (AR) Focused on Literacy**	■ Principals and literacy leadership teams model the exploration of school literacy data to determine areas of students' strength and need.	■ Principals and literacy leadership teams share data with staff and discuss teaching outcomes necessary to increase achievement for all students.	■ District PL is provided to guide staff to focus on developing one research question that they need to know more about, based on multiple data sets. ■ Time is set aside throughout the year for discussion focused on finding answers to the AR question—an example of accountable staff talk.	■ The district gives money for in-school PL days to consolidate findings in order to answer and write report on AR question. ■ All teachers committed to applying discussed assessment and instruction approaches needed to answer AR question to ensure that all students are learning.

(Continued)

Figure 5.2 (Continued)

PARAMETER	MODELED PRACTICE	SHARED PRACTICE	GUIDED PRACTICE	INTERDEPENDENT PRACTICE
12. **Parental Involvement**	■ Everyone models the belief that parents are students' first and most important teachers: sending us their best for us to ensure that they reach their potential.	■ Principals and teachers reach out to the community to bring parents in to schools. ■ Schools host adult learning session day/night. ■ Use of technology and software to learn at home is supported through take-home programs.	■ Principals and teachers are able to confidently articulate to parents and the community why, what, and how they do in the classrooms.	■ Parents and students know what, why, and how students are doing and have a clear understanding of learning expectations and what students need to do to reach the next learning level.
13. **Cross-Curricular Literacy**	■ The language of the discipline is modeled in every subject area. ■ Modeled, shared, guided, and independent approaches are used to differentiate instruction and scaffold literacy learning in all subjects.	■ Discussion groups, demonstration classrooms, video streaming, and web technologies are used to share examples of cross-curricular instruction for all teachers.	■ Curriculum consultants, literacy coaches, and knowledgeable others work alongside classroom teachers to integrate literacy into all subject areas.	■ Students experience that the taught, learned, and assessed curriculum align. ■ Students make connections to text as media and media as text. ■ Students work collaboratively online, building projects together.
14. **Shared Responsibility and Accountability**	■ The focused literacy priority of the province, district, school, and classroom is aligned, clear, precise, and intentional. ■ Everyone knows and can articulate the priority.	■ All elementary and secondary school teams participate in evidence-based literacy improvement presentations at district Literacy Learning Fair.	■ All schools host their own Literacy Learning Fairs for parents and community members. ■ Teams of teachers present their AR findings at Literacy Learning Fairs	■ The case management approach (Parameter 6), with time during the day, is available to any teacher who is struggling to reach a student; teachers and administrators, assisted by

■ The priority is clearly reflected in the AR question developed (Parameter 11) in every school using triangulation of data.	■ Principals and teachers conduct nonevaluative literacy walks together to ask reflective questions about practice that goes deeper. ■ Classroom teachers open doors to each other, making practice public.	that evidence increased students' literacy achievement. ■ Streaming technology is used to make the Literacy Learning Fairs accessible to the broader community. ■ All teachers use data to drive differentiated instruction. ■ Assessment data is delivered to administrators' and teachers' desktops, making everyone accountable and responsible for putting individual student faces on the data and taking action for all students. ■ Principals and teachers conduct nonevaluative literacy walks together, which result in coaching conversations to go deeply into practice that supports all students' achievement.	colleagues, find assessment and instructional strategies that work with each student brought forward (and continue until they do), thus becoming accountable and responsible for all students. ■ Students, facilitated by teachers, present at Literacy Learning Fairs in their schools and can articulate to parents and the broader community why they have improved in literacy and what the next steps will be; they show how their work is connected to the district work at the district Literacy Learning Fairs. ■ Students and teachers develop Sharepoint or other technology to communicate their achievements continuously to those beyond their schools (superintendents, community members, trustees, etc.). ■ Coaching conversations focused on increasing student achievement occur throughout the school day by all staff and students who make classrooms public places of learning.

CHAPTER SIX

The 14th Parameter

14 Parameters

1. Shared beliefs and understandings

2. Embedded literacy coaches

3. Time-tabled literacy block

4. Principal leadership

5. Early and ongoing intervention

6. Case management approach

7. Literacy professional development at school staff meetings

8. In-school grade/subject meetings

9. Book rooms with leveled books and resources

10. Allocation of district and school budgets for literacy learning and resources

11. Action research focused on literacy

12. Parental involvement

13. Cross-curricular literacy connections

14. Shared responsibility and accountability

(L. Sharratt & Fullan, 2005, 2006, 2009)

The 14th parameter is about whole-system accountability. Who is responsible and accountable for realization in all schools at all levels? In the past decade, we have increasingly focused on trilevel reform—school, district, and state. So far this book has centered on the first two levels of the work in a large multicultural district. Capacity building with a focus on increased student literacy achievement for all has occurred in all 192 schools of the York Region District School Board (YRDSB) and is consistently reinforced within schools, across schools (through the Literacy Learning Fair, networks, and site visits), and between schools and the district (the comprehensive literacy implementation known as the Literacy Collaborative).

In 1999, the focus was on identifying and implementing what turned out to be 13 core parameters (see Chapter 2) that establish the focused learning environment. The process, while not linear, progressed through modeled, shared, guided, and finally interdependent practice. In each phase, more and more people became involved. Ownership shifted from leader led to learner led until it became a fully developed interdependent phenomenon whereby leadership came from all levels in the district. All 192 schools are now engaged in this interdependent practice. In Chapter 5, we cited the example of Crosby Heights PS and its principal. In this chapter, we present a second example to further illustrate the powerful impact of not only the 13 parameters when they are fully implemented by a knowledgeable and highly skilled leader but also the energy created by the 14th parameter in action.

Jill Maar is the principal of Armadale Public School, the district's largest elementary school, serving a highly diverse and multilingual community. Using the parameter self-assessment tool developed by Sharratt and her district curriculum staff (see Resource A as an example), Jill and her school leadership team developed and implemented a plan of action based on the following nine components:

1. Improve the learning conditions: clean, organized, bright, well-lit plant. Regular maintenance and urgent repairs were needed in some areas because structure guides school behavior (Parameter 4).

2. Give access to current and inclusive resources: clearing out classrooms of all school-based resources (some were well stocked with resources dating back to the 1970s, while others had very few resources) through centralization across the

school; creating a literacy room, math room, science room, including text resources, technology software, and math manipulatives (Parameters 9 and 10).

3. Centralize and streamline budget decisions: developing a clear and transparent process to address essential needs and division/teacher accountability (Parameter 10).

4. Examine data and identify trends; reshape teacher thinking about the importance of data when making instructional decisions (e.g., at-risk identification, case management approach; Parameters 6 and 1).

5. Engage district curriculum consultant experts: facilitate professional learning based on teacher need and ensure consistency of practice within and across grades, for example, they assist in implementing the First 20 Days (Fountas & Pinnell, 2001), daily literacy walks in every classroom throughout the school, targeted long range and unit planning, and class meetings (Parameters 1 and 11).

6. Strategically build a leadership team: support implementation and share in the building of a school plan with SMART goal language (specific, measurable, attainable, results-based, time-bound; "What Are Smart Goals?" 2007; Parameters 2, 7, and 11).

7. Renew focus on parent and family engagement: extended library hours, parent/family town hall sessions, street festivals, and heritage and English language classes (Parameter 12).

8. Attend to early and ongoing interventions: kindergarten/ Grade 1 programs focus on oral language and use of the Reading Recovery Observation Survey as a valuable assessment tool to guide instruction (Parameter 5).

9. Hold our nerve: protecting instructional time, honoring the literacy block, and designating specific time to meet in school to discuss program needs and students' increased literacy achievement (Parameters 3, 8, and 13).

Jill is a dedicated instructional leader who as lead-learner—with will and perseverance—is a living example of how the 13 parameters can bring support and focus to every administrator and teacher in every school. Jill demonstrates modeled, shared, and guided practice when necessary, not lock-step but in concert, matching the parameters at the right time with the varied needs of her staff. Jill is an interdependent leader who understands how to bring all the parameters to life in a school with 890 students and 67 staff members. The answer lies in the 14th parameter—shared responsibility and accountability—and Jill's narrative below demonstrates how to reflect and integrate the parameters in order to increase literacy achievement for each student.

Accountability and Responsibility at Armadale Public School: An Example of the 14th Parameter

Our sense of urgency to improve student achievement for all students while closing the achievement gap for at-risk students crystallized after analyzing a variety of data sources. As a team, we needed to firmly establish our shared beliefs and understandings to ensure that *all* teachers can support *all* students in reaching *high* expectations in *all* subject areas (Hill & Crévola, 1999). Initial student gains have been achieved, as evidenced in the latest data collected both qualitatively and quantitatively.

Jill reports that her team has collaboratively set high expectations for the literacy learning of both teachers and students. In taking responsibility for implementing the parameters, they have achieved the following:

- Job-embedded professional learning, based on student needs, has increased the consistency of practice within and among classrooms. Teachers are beginning to model lessons in one another's classrooms on a monthly basis, thereby building capacity and understanding.
- Professional learning is active in each division. The identified focus is assessment-based instruction with teacher moderation of student work.
- Teachers are using a variety of assessment tools and instructional strategies to meet the learning styles, interests, and needs of every student.
- Teachers are building class and student profiles and attending case management sessions to identify high-yield strategies.

- Teachers and students can clearly articulate what the learning targets are and what success criteria are needed in order to achieve the targets, as evidenced through daily literacy walks.
- Two teams (of five teachers each) are engaged in action research and meet bimonthly to review their data, actions, and research.
- Ninety-eight percent of the staff have volunteered to participate in a biweekly professional book club and bring supporting student evidence to their discussions.
- An increase in the usage and frequency of centralized resources has been acknowledged through not only centralized tracking systems but also the observations and comments of teachers and students who are accessing them.
- Student needs are at the forefront when making budget decisions with grade/divisional teams.
- Attendance at family/community school events has increased by 200 percent (School Council sessions have grown from 8 members to 67; Early Years parent sessions on average have 48 to 50 parents attending now on a regular basis).

The quantitative data also confirm that by continuing to improve learning conditions, celebrating collaborative practices, and sustaining a climate of trust and transparency, students are beginning to show performance gains (see Figure 6.1).

Figure 6.1 shows significant reduction in the number of students at risk in kindergarten through Grade 5—especially those at Level 1—in one year of intense, focused activity. While the at-risk numbers still need to be improved further, Jill considers the skill sets used in kindergarten–Grade 5 interventions to be necessary in Grades 6 to 8, and she will train or move staff to provide for that increased instructional capacity. What is impressive is that Jill knows every student and has her finger on the performance pulse at Armadale. She is able to provide up-to-the-minute assessment results for each student. She and her teachers can name the at-risk students individually and clearly articulate what they are doing for each one. We believe that this is the essence of the 14th parameter. In implementing all of the parameters, including the 14th, Jill has daily conversations with teachers and works alongside them to coplan and coteach. She is truly an evidence-based, knowledgeable, and passionate leader.

Figure 6.1 Summary of Armadale Students Identified as At Risk in Reading*

| | | October 2008 Planning Process | | | | February 2009 Planning Process | | |
| | | Number of Students At Risk | | | | Number of Students At Risk | | |
Grade	Enrollment October 2008	Level 1 or Below	Level 2	Total At Risk	Enrollment February 2009	Level 1 or Below	Level 2	Total At Risk
Kindergarten	75	68	0	68	77	11	35	46
1	92	42	13	55	83	29	17	46
2	94	23	28	51	87	11	23	34
3	82	26	14	40	78	8	21	29
4	70	7	15	22	70	6	12	18
5	83	14	26	40	83	7	26	33
6	106	11	24	35	107	5	29	34
7	87	14	19	33	86	14	17	31
8	109	18	16	34	108	17	20	37
Total	798	223	155	378 (47%)	779	108	202	233 (30%)

* "At risk" defined as Level 2 or below on a 4-point scale.

89

Even if a system has established a vision and an infrastructure of support (e.g., through professional learning sessions about the 13 parameters offered by the district and aligned and restated in learning networks), the presence of accountable and responsible leaders demonstrates that good leaders can accelerate the pace of progress.

In the rest of this chapter we consider what it would take to implement the 14th parameter: strategies for achieving accountability and responsibility for realization at the district and then state (whole-system) levels.

REALIZATION AT THE DISTRICT LEVEL

The 13 parameters concern the day-to-day implementation of deepened capacity building, with a focus on literacy and associated achievement for all students. This is done through job-embedded professional learning with school teams, reinforced by all schools within clusters and networks, and guided by district leaders. All of this is further buttressed by leadership development; careful selection of leaders; and support of aspiring, newly appointed, and continuing school leaders (YRDSB, 2007b). As we have shown, this more focused day-to-day assessment and instructional practice dovetails with nonstop personal development.

The glue that holds this together and a key strategic element of the 14th parameter is the annual live report of evidence related to student achievement. It is critical to note that this is not an exercise in bureaucratic accountability reporting. Put one way, we did not start with accountability but rather ended with it. Put still another way, after all schools were steeped in capacity building, we sought a natural re-enforcer that integrated accountability and responsibility and fed more positive energy into the cycle at the school level.

Interdependent leadership practice and the 14th parameter are evident in the Literacy Learning Fair held each spring in York Region. All 192 elementary and secondary schools prepare a half-hour multimedia presentation based on the following:

- What the school set out to do that year
- Evidence to support students' increased literacy achievement
- What assessment and instructional strategies were used
- Lessons learned
- The challenges that the school is currently facing

What is most impressive when observing the Literacy Learning Fair is how articulate, consistent, and specific YRDSB educators have become when they discuss the what, the why, the how, and the assessed impact of their work. Every school in the district participates in teams; in other words, there are over one thousand change agents spread across 192 schools, all engaged in the same phenomenon—using precise language to push practice to the next level.

Every school administrator and teacher team prepares an evidenced-based report (focused on student data), then submits it to their superintendents and the district. The reports show their improved school results and intentional next steps for the following year that are to be incorporated in their updated school improvement plans. Low-performing leaders are supported, pulled along, and energized in this process by strong leaders who reach out.

In the early stages, it was intended that these presentations would be precise and instructive to their internal school audiences and to those from the other schools initially involved in the research. Much later, when the entire school district embraced the 13 parameters, the annual reporting served as a collaborative dialogue across schools and deepened participants' understanding of their own individual and the collective learning, which led to generating additional next steps to be taken in their schools. It also broadened the interdependency from intraschool to interschool, with one critical result being a reduction in the overall performance gap between schools.

Since our research, the preparation and presenting of schools' annual improvement reports have become cause for celebration and open recognition within and across schools in this district. At the end of each school year, a day is set aside for the Literacy Learning Fair so that administrators and teachers (three from each elementary and secondary school) can come together to make oral and visual presentations of their reports to other school teams. In this way, everyone has been able to learn from other schools' successes—and from their "what not to do" learning as well. School teams and district leaders have embedded the reporting as an operating norm, not just an expectation. Teams leave the Literacy Learning Fair inspired and with renewed energy to achieve even more for and with their students in the following school year.

Now all YRDSB schools have their literacy leadership teams involved in the Literacy Learning Fair. However, the 14th parameter demands that not only must literacy leadership teams participate in the district's fair, but all schools must host their own annual Literacy Learning Fairs, with all classes—teachers as well as students—reporting to parents and the community on the evidence that demonstrates the improvement of all students. This end-to-end reporting and the resulting presentations demonstrate that the 14 parameters (see Figure 6.2) lead to interdependence—ongoing, sustainable growth in academic achievement for all students. This is the accountability that realization demands and breeds—accountability to and responsibility for one another.

The 14th parameter not only answers the responsibility and accountability question at school and district levels by ensuring reporting on strengthened classroom practice for all students, but also sends definitive feedback concerning school improvement and individual student achievement to the province/state that is responsible and accountable for state/provincial budgets and overall increased student achievement.

CAPACITY BUILDING TO REALIZATION: AN OVERVIEW

Does realization negate the importance of initiating capacity-building measures? To the contrary, you can't get there without it. But as we have said throughout this book, it does signal that our work has only just begun. Pulling out teacher and administrator leadership teams to participate in professional development programs is only a small beginning that will introduce shared beliefs and understandings, common language, and knowledge transfer only among those present. The real journey starts when learning becomes the work. Systemic capacity building is incomplete until the realization phase during which self-reflection and self-assessment at every level drive changed instructional practices, delivering consistent experiences to every classroom, in all schools, for every student across a district (interdependent practice and the 14th parameter!).

Realization is a much more sophisticated, systematic approach to deepening district-wide reform that becomes systemic, self-sustaining, and unstoppable. We know that it requires on-the-ground expertise in every school, expertise that is precisely matched at province/state and district levels with authentic leaders who understand not only successful instructional practices but also strategic timing—a collective commitment to knowing when to do the right thing and how to do the right things right in order to move a system and its schools forward. It is a focused mobilization against inertia.

Will, perseverance, and trust building are necessary inputs as well as positive outcomes of realization; figuring out what the right things are, finding out how to do them right, and then doing the right things right, everywhere—and being capable of repeating this process every school year—is realization.

Figure 6.2 reflects this thinking and shows that working on the 13 parameters creates a successful professional and student learning environment that leads to embracing all 14 parameters as clearly articulated, evidence-based self-actualization, which results in interdependent practice, or realization. Although linear in representation, this work is not lock-step—denoting that every system, leader, and teacher must self-assess against all 14 parameters to find starting points for their learning in each parameter. Figure 6.2 depicts the importance of scaffolding learning from modeled to shared to guided to interdependent practice, as we

Figure 6.2 Capacity Building to Realization

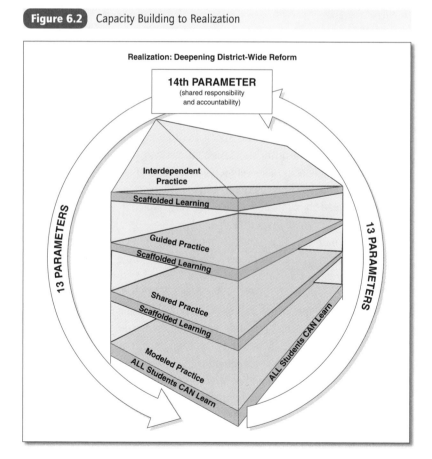

have described in detail in this book. The importance of wrapping around our progressive learning model with the 13 parameters and attaining self-actualization in the 14th parameter is as foundational to understand as is our basic premise—that all students can learn. This model applies across all contexts in every state, district, school, and classroom.

The following vignette is authentic in all its detail and represents an especially poignant and passionate demonstration of how all 14 parameters working together seamlessly and in concert can successfully increase student achievement.

Vignette: Tiger's Story Culminates in Achieving Realization (All 14 Parameters in Action!)

Tiger, a six-year-old student with Down's syndrome, loved school and attended Grade 1 regularly. It was September and time for the teacher to assess students, using Running Records and the Observation Survey (Reading Recovery) tools, to make a data-driven decision to identify the four lowest-performing children in his class. These children would then receive Reading Recovery. The teacher said, "This one, this one, this one, but not this one—Tiger—as he will never learn to read." The principal agreed, as did the Reading Recovery teacher; however, she knew she needed to check it out with the Reading Recovery teacher-leader to find out if this decision reflected the district's vision/beliefs and understandings.

Months later, at a district school board meeting, an item on the agenda was the annual Reading Recovery report. Hazel, teacher-leader and principal of the Reading Recovery program, began: "This is the story of how Tiger learned to read through the Reading Recovery program. At first no one felt that he would or could learn to read."

At that moment, Tiger and his mom came in to the board meeting. Superintendent Sharratt went over to quietly welcome them. Then Tiger confidently read a story (in the mid–Grade 1 range) to the board of trustees, the director, the superintendents, and a room full of adults. The teacher-leader had worked with the school staff all year to build their understandings of the meaning of "all students" (and had supported the Reading Recovery teacher with her initial concerns by providing mentoring and coaching to start Tiger's lessons). Tiger was obviously delighted with his newly acquired reading skills. His mom took Sharratt up on her offer to say a few words to the board. She began, faltering, "Thank you for believing in Tiger, for believing that all children can learn. I hope all parents of struggling early learners have the opportunity that my boy had to learn to read. Thank you so much." There wasn't a dry eye in the board room as Tiger stood up proudly for his bow, waving to everyone after a round of applause for him, for his resiliency in learning to read, and for Reading Recovery foundational values that encouraged educators to believe in him and in all children.

For all of us, Tiger's reading was living proof that our vision was the correct one: all children can and will learn.

REALIZATION AT THE STATE OR PROVINCE LEVEL

In 2003, with a newly elected provincial government, we had the opportunity to strive for realization for the entire Ontario public school system (there is no federal involvement in K–12 education in Canada). One of us (Fullan) was appointed as the premier's special advisor on education. The new premier, Dalton McGuinty, positioned himself as the education premier. He faced a stagnant school system (literacy and numeracy achievement had been flat for five years) and a demoralized principal and teaching force. Using some of the principles of capacity building and realization, the province set about to improve the entire system—two million students in four thousand elementary and nine hundred secondary schools in 72 districts.

Certainly, the YRDSB leaders informed many of the specifics of the strategy, but the overall approach also benefited from the work of other successful districts in the province and from the experience in the United Kingdom in which Tony Blair and his government designed a similar strategy to improve literacy and numeracy there during the 1997–2001 period.

It is beyond our scope in this book to detail the Ontario strategy (see Fullan, 2009a; Levin, 2008; Levin, Glaze, & Fullan, 2008). Essentially the province's strategy involved the following:

- Establishing a small number of core, ambitious goals (improvement in literacy, numeracy, and high school graduation rates)
- Setting performance targets that were jointly negotiated between schools/districts and the government
- Investing heavily in capacity building by establishing a provincial Literacy and Numeracy Secretariat to support schools and districts in developing their own capacities such as impleenting the 13 parameters

- Employing strategies for schools and districts to learn from each other during implementation
- Targeting attention to key underperforming groups, including minority students, ESL students, students in special education, aboriginal students, and boys
- Designing and supporting effective use of data to track students and intervene when problems occur
- Supporting ancillary practice, such as expansion of tutoring and fuller engagement of parents and communities
- Having a nonpunitive turnaround strategy for schools that was based on capacity building rather than blame

There are more specifics and more detail, but the strategy was framed around three big sustaining elements:

- Respect for staff and for professional knowledge
- Comprehensiveness
- Coherence and alignment through partnership (Levin et al., 2008, p. 278)

Now in its fifth year (the government was reelected in 2007), the strategy is working. Literacy and numeracy achievement has risen 11 percent in the elementary schools, high school graduation rates have increased from 68 percent to 77 percent, teacher and principal morale has been boosted, and parents are more satisfied.

Ontario by no means has reached sustainable realization (nor has YRDSB). We are discovering that the closer you get to it and the more you work on it, the more you grasp that this is a relentless, never-ending, often vulnerable journey. Gains are made and consolidated, but you must stay the course; you can never let up. Relentless focus and detailed, systematic capacity building that lead to realization are enduring features of large organizations and systems pursuing sustainable learning (Fullan, 2009a).

Finally, it should be noted that such systematic action on the part of the province/state in the study by Leithwood and colleagues (2009) was conspicuous in its absence. Those researchers found that "because few states have comprehensive approaches to reform, state agencies and school districts are provided with general directions but limited guidance on how to achieve the goal of improving student learning" (p. 139). This is certainly not the case in Ontario, and York Region and the other 71 districts are better off for it. And so is the province as it learns from the best districts. Whole-system change, because it requires a combination of top-down, bottom-up, and lateral forces, is a two-way street as people learn from each other.

REALIZATION IS A SUSTAINABLE FUTURE

It is our contention that while individual leaders and teachers can and must work on their own sustainable growth in classroom achievement, the conditions for sustaining large numbers of people as they adopt a progressive learning model can only be fostered if the educational system as a whole is working in this direction. Moreover, we maintain that focusing on sustainable growth in classroom achievement must become more deliberate, and directions toward it must be very precise. At the very least, annual measurement and articulation of student achievement must become an operating norm at every level (the 14th parameter). Sustainable growth in classroom achievement needs explicit attention—it must be worked on in a self-conscious and organizationally conscious manner. All of the elements serve simultaneously as strategies for both improvement and responsible accountability. Thus, realization is achieved when teachers and leaders at every level do the following:

1. Clearly understand the progressive model we present here and, most important, live the priority—the shared beliefs and understandings underpinning it.

2. Continuously engage in dialogue, reflection, and self-assessment, striving to align behavior, beliefs, and practice among province/state, districts, schools, and classrooms.

3. Do not let distracters divert the focus and energy from the priority. Teachers' and leaders' energy is recharged when they experience their own improvement and the improvement of their students.

4. Hear the same mantra of the singular, unassailable focus on increasing students' literacy achievement from the province/state, district, and school leaders.

5. Engage in purposeful interaction within and across schools, and become more aware of, and indeed more committed to, the success of other schools and students in addition to their own.

The key concepts pertain to whether the system goes about its work in ways that

- help people throughout the system and beyond focus on the priority;
- motivate and energize people to make investments that are sensitive to the ebb and flow of energies;
- use teachers' and students' success to beget more success;
- create a critical mass of leaders and teachers who work on these very matters to engage and commit everyone to focus together;
- provide system supports to surround and ensure the realization of the 14 parameters (see Resource B);
- continually assess whether the 14 parameters are occurring consistently and deeply;
- make haste slowly—go fast enough to make progress but not so fast as to allow missteps in executing any of the 14 parameters, which would trip up overall progress or sustainability.

ENSURING REALIZATION BEYOND TODAY

I continue to work with principals (who I see as pivotal) and school superintendents (who are underutilized as instructional leaders) in terms of planning, observations, and feedback. We explore what the indicators and observable "look-fors" are, what data are gathered and how they are used; we ask how do you know what it is that you're seeing, what are the critical conversations to have with staff, and what does feedback that makes a difference sound like?

(Bev Freedman, Educational Consultant, personal communication, September 2008)

Many of our colleagues have their own ways of expressing what they are doing to sustain realization beyond their tenure. Many speak of setting up networks across districts and schools to support and learn from one another. Robyn Welch, from the Ontario Literacy and Numeracy Secretariat, says, "What we're finding across the province is that sustainability is difficult—it's a marathon, not a sprint, so all conditions must support this hard work. . . . Everyone at every level has to be engaged and take responsibility for students' success and well-being."

Leaders who have been working toward realization for a very

long time believe that it is sustained through individual, focused support as well as a broadly accepted focus. They mention purposeful, coherent, and aligned practice, consistent from class to class, that is energizing and not stagnant (Judy Speirs, Senior Student Achievement Officer, Ontario Literacy and Numeracy Secretariat, personal communication, August 2008). Superintendents in all 72 districts must be aligned in their actions and personally involved in the improvement of assessment and instruction with the administrators and teachers in all of their schools.

Several colleagues mention inclusive reworked structures, which include representatives (that have authentic voice) from all levels in the organization to help foster collaboratively made decisions and ensure thoughtful plans for continuous improvement—always focused on student achievement. Many have found ways to have overlapping roles so that there are no huge gaps when system leaders leave.

Others mention the importance of finding "bright lights" and mentoring them to take on new roles in order to have a seamless transition when leaders and teachers leave. Others have already thought about their exit and have nurtured and groomed teacher-leaders to take over, knowing

Our senior team has supported a collective model of literacy support, and in the event that any one of us should leave, the model would survive. . . . Program services must be able to support field superintendents and schools in achieving our collective literacy goals. We have made several changes to the way we operate so that we ensure that literacy is THE fundamental priority. Our system plan now reflects this, and our superintendent team fully supports it. We are excited!

(Laura Elliott, Program Superintendent, Thames Valley District School Board, personal communication, August 2008)

I have been working on sustainability of the Reading Recovery Program for at least 3 years—mentoring others and sharing a variety of different tasks, and encouraging promising people with a variety of different strengths and styles to join the team. Still working on this one—and working on sharing the learning of the past 15 years so that there can be a seamless transition. The big hurdle I see is the implicit knowledge needed—the strategic thinking to continue to ensure that the work continues in changing contexts.

(Hazel Dick, Curriculum Administrator, Reading Recovery Program, York Region District School Board, personal communication, August 2008)

that it is human nature to revert back to old ways unless pressed on by someone who has been part of the direction-setting (Laurie Welch, Principal, Victor Lauriston School, Chatham, Ontario, personal communication, October 2008). Again they are hoping for that overlap necessary to honor what has already been achieved and that demands an understanding of how to stay the course. We have found that systems that are approaching a state of realization have carefully thought about sustainability of direction and succession planning for all positions, thus eliminating the chaos created when surprises occur.

Over many years of working together, we have been able to identify some of the main themes of sustainability of realization. They amount to focus, consistency, mutual alignment, and reinforcement of purpose among the province/state, district, and school levels; staying the course; and developing an attitude that continuity of good direction in increasing student achievement is paramount. We know sustainability, as in continuous effort and energy, is always vulnerable. We know that creating and sustaining a positive learning culture requires a lot of work. We recognize that a positive learning culture can be destroyed quickly with a change in leadership and/or political conditions that do not instantly model a commitment to stay the course. Yet by making what works explicit through the progressive learning model we present, and by enabling more and more leaders at all levels to be aware of and maintain the conditions that energize them and those with whom they work, the chances for sustaining the positive learning culture, and therefore realization, are greatly enhanced.

> Real buy-in and authentic change exist when our tenure in a school ends, yet the elements of our core beliefs continue to flourish because teachers realize what the real work is all about and are disciplined practitioners. They have posed the reflective questions and know the rationale for what they do.
>
> (Greg Farrell, Principal, Louis-Honore Frechette Public School, personal communication, September 2008)

In short, it is not so much that people need to believe that realization is possible, but more that they need to acknowledge that it is the only way to move forward and be "in the game"—to be fully engaged, seeking and helping to develop leaders and teachers whose core beliefs are focused on the notions that all leaders can and will lead every teacher, all teachers can and will teach every child, and all students can and will learn. Above all, people must experience the value of realization. There is no greater motivation to keep going than getting results on critical moral matters.

20 Years to Begin Large-Scale Reform

It was in 1988 that the first examples of district-wide reform began. District 2 in New York City was one of the first documented cases of systematic, instructionally focused, whole-district successes (Elmore & Burney, 1999). It was also in 1988 that we created the Learning Consortium in Ontario—a partnership between the university and four large urban districts—which focused on school and district improvement.

A decade of work later, we were ready to begin more systematic work on district-wide reform. The occasion was pinpointing the literacy priority followed by establishing the Literacy Collaborative in York Region District School Board, which is largely the account presented in this book. From 1999 to the present, we have learned a great deal about changing almost two hundred schools simultaneously. This journey toward realization consists of the four big-picture orientations (shared vision, focused assessment and instruction, strategic leadership, and parent and community engagement), the 13 parameters, and the four scaffolded building blocks of practice (modeling, sharing, guiding, and interdependent) and culminates with the 14th wraparound parameter (shared responsibility and accountability).

Pioneering journeys are slow at the beginning. But once basic know-how is established, and as talented and kindred spirits grow in numbers, the flashpoints of progress become ubiquitous and inevitable. We believe that a sense of professional urgency, know-how, and facilitation skills are currently merging among leaders, teachers, union officials, and communities that are under attack by the stress of tremendous economic pressures and increasingly strident demands for improved performance on a global stage. The result will be accelerated, deep, large-scale reform—at district as well as whole-system levels (states, provinces, countries).

Whole-system reform is increasingly becoming the focus for many countries around the world (Schleicher, 2009). In the United States, state governors and the new federal administration under President Obama and Secretary of State Arne Duncan are now searching for best practices that increase the capacity of educators to raise the bar and close the gap for all students. The massive influx of new so-called stimulus money (over $100 billion) via the American Reinvestment and Recovery Act signals a new era for deliberate, more comprehensive whole-system strategies. The No Child Left Behind federal legislation will be revamped to reflect these new realities and corresponding strategies.

Our book clearly shows what will be needed on the ground. It will require the focused and comprehensive efforts that we describe in detail here that build capacity and lead to sustained realization. We know a great deal about how to do this. Realization provides a clear foundation and building blocks for whole-state/province reform.

The next one to five years will be telling. For the first time, we have grounded confidence that effective large-scale reform is within our grasp. Realizing district-wide reform is a critical beginning. The next step, whole-state/province reform (Fullan, 2009b), is something that could not be imaginable in the absence of the foundational knowledge experienced and described in this book. Successful large-scale reform has become a reality!

Resource A

A Tool for Assessing Implementation of the 14 Parameters: Selected Examples

We have learned over three years that success of increased literacy achievement for our students is dependent on the consistent implementation of 13 critical parameters (L. Sharratt & Fullan, 2005), and we add the 14th parameter in this book. The following are excerpts from a self-assessment tool developed by L. Sharratt and curriculum colleagues from 2005 to 2008.

1. Shared Beliefs and Understandings	Implementation Scale	Next Steps
1. **Shared Beliefs and Understandings** • All students can achieve high standards, given sufficient time and the right support. • High expectations and early and ongoing intervention are essential. • All teachers can teach to high standards given the right assistance. • Teachers can articulate what they do and why they teach the way they do.	1 ⊢————————⊣ 5 Awareness Full Implementation	

13. Cross-Curricular Literacy Connections	Implementation Scale	Next Steps
The components of balanced literacy instruction are evident, and teachers support students in developing meaning-making skills in all subject disciplines. • Assessment data determine what literacy skills students will need to develop in order to access the content of the discipline across all grades and courses. • Teachers in all content areas further student achievement in literacy by modeling skills, doing think-alouds to share their thinking, guiding students toward independent thinking, and monitoring their progress on an individual basis.	1 5 Awareness Full Implementation	

14. Shared Responsibility and Accountability	Implementation Scale	Next Steps
• Triangulation of data informs the professional learning needed in district and schools. • Ongoing use of formative data provides descriptive feedback for students, differentiates instruction, and impacts the selection of resources. • The district disaggregates and delivers data to administrators' and teachers' desktops to put individual faces on the data and assists in the development of improvement plans to collaboratively take action. • Administrators and teachers can name at-risk students individually and clearly articulate what they are doing for each one. • School staffs work on finding results of action research question based on schools' data. • The district hosts an evidence-based Literacy Learning Fair for all school teams to share student improvement and learn from other schools. • Schools host their own Literacy Learning Fairs for parents and the community.	1 5 Awareness Full Implementation	

Resource B

10 District Supports That Evolved to Ensure
Realization of All Parameters

1. Reading Recovery (fully implemented in every school that has a primary division)

2. Literacy Content Sessions (focused on assessment, instruction, and balanced literacy in all classrooms)

3. District Change Management Sessions (led by curriculum department with external research partners)

4. Networked Learning Sessions (led by field superintendents and curriculum staff, with the goal of reaching all teachers)

5. Action Research (training to establish whole-school collaborative inquiry using data to develop a focusing question)

6. Intensive Support Schools (identified by data, supported by curriculum consultant staff, and provided with additional resources focused on needs)

7. Demonstration Classrooms (Literacy@School: open for visitors to see how literacy and technology are integrated seamlessly during the school day)

8. Literacy Walks and Coaching Conversations (district training sessions led by district principal responsible for literacy and a curriculum consultant)

9. Afterschool Professional Learning Sessions (for classroom teachers and supply teachers who are unable to attend sessions during the day)

10. Literacy Learning Fairs (hosted by the district and schools)

References

Allen, R. (2003, Summer). Expanding writing's role in learning: Teacher training holds key to change. *Curriculum Update,* 1–2.

Anderson, S. (2006). The school district role in educational change. *International Journal of Educational Reform, 15*(1), 13–37.

Barber, M. (2003, November). *Literacy: "I'm in favour of it."* Keynote address at the Quest for Literacy Conference, Richmond Hill, Ontario, Canada.

Belchetz, D. (2004). *Successful leadership practices in an accountable policy context: Influence on student achievement.* Unpublished doctoral dissertation, University of Toronto, Toronto, Ontario, Canada.

Claxton, G. (2002). *Building learning power.* Bristol, England: TLO.

Clay, M. (2005). *Literacy lessons part 1.* Portsmouth, NH: Heinemann.

Cross City Campaign for Urban School Reform. (2005). *A delicate balance: District policies and classroom practice.* Chicago: Author.

Datoo, S. (2006). *An analysis and comparison of R. Friedman's leadership and Hall and Hord's 12 principles that embody the concern's-based approach to implementing changes.* Unpublished manuscript, University of Toronto, Toronto, Ontario, Canada.

Elmore, R. (2004). *School reform from the inside out.* Cambridge, MA: Harvard Education Press.

Elmore, R., & Burney, D. (1999). Investing in teacher learning. In L. Darling-Hammond & G. Sykes (Eds.), *Teaching as the learning profession* (pp. 236–291). San Francisco: Jossey-Bass.

Epstein, J. (1995). School/family/community partnerships: Caring for the children we share. *Phi Delta Kappan, 76,* 701–712.

Fountas, I., & Pinnell, G. S. (2001). *Guiding readers and writers: Grades 3–6.* Portsmouth, NH: Heinemann.

Franklin, J. (2003, Summer). Breaking the barriers: How writing across the curriculum programs help students and teachers. *Curriculum Update,* 4–5.

Fullan, M. (2003). *Change forces with a vengeance.* London: Routledge Falmer.

Fullan, M. (2007). *The new meaning of educational change* (4th ed.). New York: Teachers College Press.

Fullan, M. (2008). *The six secrets of change.* San Francisco: Jossey-Bass.

Fullan, M. (2009a). Have theory will travel: A theory of action for system change. In A. Hargreaves & M. Fullan (Eds.), *Change wars* (pp. 275–293). Bloomington, IN: Solution Tree.

Fullan, M. (2009b). Large-scale reform comes of age. *Journal of Educational Change, 10,* 101–113.

Fullan, M., Hill, P., & Crévola, C. (2006). *Breakthrough.* Thousand Oaks, CA: Corwin.

Fullan, M., & Sharratt, L. (2007). Sustaining leadership in complex times: An individual and system solution. In B. Davies (Ed.), *Developing sustainable leadership* (pp. 116–136). London: Sage.

Gladwell, M. (2008). *Outliers: The story of success.* New York: Little, Brown.

Hill, P. W., & Crévola, C. A. (1999). The role of standards in educational reform for the 21st century. In D. D. Marsh (Ed.), *ASCD yearbook 1999: Preparing our schools for the 21st century* (pp. 117–42). Alexandria, VA: Association for Supervision and Curriculum Development.

Hubbard, L., Mehan, H., & Stein, M. K. (2006). *Reform as learning: School reform, organizational culture, and community politics in San Diego.* London: Routledge.

Leithwood, K., Leonard, L., & Sharratt, L. (2000). Conditions fostering organizational learning in schools. In K. Leithwood (Ed.), *Understanding schools as intelligent systems* (pp. 99–124). Stamford, CT: JAI Press.

Leithwood, K., Louis, K. S., Wahlstrom, K., Anderson, S., Mascall, B., Michlin, M., et al. (2009). *Learning from district efforts to improve student achievement.* New York: Wallace Foundation.

Levin, B. (2008). *How to change 5000 schools.* Cambridge, MA: Harvard Education Press.

Levin, B., Glaze, A., & Fullan, M. (2008). Results without rancor or ranking: Ontario's success story. *Phi Delta Kappan, 90,* 273–280.

Lewin, K. (1967). *Resolving social conflicts.* New York: Harper & Row.

Lewis, C. C. (2002). *Lesson study: A handbook of teacher-led instructional change.* Philadelphia: Research for Better Schools.

The long-term costs of literacy difficulties. (2006). London: KPMG Foundation.

Meek, M. (1991). *On being literate.* Portsmouth, NH: Heinemann.

Ostinelli, G. (2008, January). *The school improvement advisor/researcher SIA: Helping the individual school in the self-management of improvement.* Paper presented at the Admee Meeting, Geneva, Switzerland.

Pfeffer, J., & Sutton, R. (2006). *Hard facts, dangerous half-truths, and total nonsense.* Boston: Harvard Business School Press.

Planche, B. (2004). *Probing the complexities of collaboration and collaborative processes.* Unpublished doctoral dissertation, University of Toronto, Toronto, Ontario, Canada.

Planche, B. (2007). *A leadership lens on the complexities of collaboration.* Unpublished report prepared for the Simcoe County (Ontario, Canada) Board of Education.

Planche, B., & Sharratt, L. (2008, November). *13 parameters for leaders leading school and system improvement.* Presentation at the Quest for Increased Student Achievement conference, Richmond Hill, Ontario, Canada.

Planche, B., Sharratt, L., & Belchetz, D. (2008, January). *Sustaining students' increased achievement through second order change: Do collaboration and leadership count?* Paper presented at the International Congress for School Effectiveness and Improvement conference, Auckland, New Zealand.

Prytula, M. P. (2008). *Scholarship epistemology: An exploratory study of teacher metacognition within the context of successful learning communities.* Unpublished doctoral dissertation, University of Saskatchewan, Saskatoon, Saskatchewan, Canada.

Reeves, D. (2007, September 10). *Teacher moderation: Collaborative assessment of student work.* Literacy and Numeracy Secretariat Webcast, Ontario, Canada.

Robertson, J. (2005). *Leadership coaching leadership: Building educational leadership capacity through leadership coaching partnerships.* Wellington, New Zealand: NZCER Press.

Rosenholtz, S. J. (1989). *Teachers' workplace: The social organization of schools.* New York: Longman.

Ryan, J. (2003). *Leading diverse schools.* Dordrecht, Netherlands: Kluwer.

Schleicher, A. (2009). International benchmarking as a lever for policy reform. In A. Hargreaves & M. Fullan (Eds.), *Change wars* (pp. 96–115). Bloomington, IN: Solution Tree Press.

Sharratt, L. (1996). *The influence of electronically available information on the stimulation of knowledge use and organizational learning in schools.* Unpublished doctoral dissertation, University of Toronto, Toronto, Ontario, Canada.

Sharratt, L. (2001). Making the most of accountability policies: Is there a role for the school district? *Orbit, 32*(1), 37–42.

Sharratt, L., & Fullan, M. (2005). The school district that did the right things right. *Voices in Urban Education, 9,* 5–13.

Sharratt, L., & Fullan, M. (2006). Accomplishing district wide reform. *Journal of School Leadership, 16,* 583–595.

Sharratt, L., & Sharratt, M. (2006). The impact of teachers' learning on students' literacy achievement. *College Quarterly, 9*(4). Retrieved June 12, 2009, from http://www.senecac.on.ca/quarterly/2006-vol09-num 04-fall/sharratt_sharratt.html

Sharratt, M. (2004). *The impact of teacher leadership on students' literacy learning.* Unpublished master's thesis, University of Toronto, Toronto, Ontario, Canada.

Supovitz, J. A. (2006). *The case for district-based reform.* Cambridge, MA: Harvard Education Press.

Togneri, W., & Anderson, S. (2003). How high poverty districts improve. *Leadership, 33*(1), 12–16.

What are SMART goals? (2007). *Tools for Schools, 11*(2), 3.

What Works Clearinghouse. (2007). *A three year study on intervention and Reading Recovery.* Washington, DC: U.S. Department of Education.

Wolchak, P. (2004, May/June). Laptops boost marks for grade-school kids. *Backbone.*

York Region District School Board. (2003–2004). *Reading Recovery site report.* Aurora, Ontario, Canada: Author.

York Region District School Board. (2007a). *Guidelines for literacy.* Aurora, Ontario, Canada: Author.

York Region District School Board. (2007b). *Leadership development plan.* Aurora, Ontario, Canada: Author.

York Region District School Board. (2007c). *Literacy walks report.* Aurora, Ontario, Canada: Author.

Index